THE BOUNCE BACK WOMAN

by

Shannon DeGarmo

THE BOUNCE BACK WOMAN

Published by Keep the Faith Publishing, a division of Big Oyo, LLC
2000 Mallory Lane, Suite 130-237
Franklin, Tennessee 37067
www.keepthefaith.com

Version KTF.001.2016.01

EDITIONS
Paperback: ISBN 978-0996300506
E-Book: ISBN 978-0996300513

Cover Design: Kim Russell/Wahoo Designs
Digital Design: Telemachus Press, LLC

International English Version

10 9 8 7 6 5 4 3 2 1

Contents

Foreword
A Healing Grace

As I turned the pages of the manuscript for *The Bounce Back Woman* late one night, I was simply amazed at the healing and grace Shannon experienced through her transparency before God, her family, and her close friends. I shed a tear for her and so many others I know who are hurting—and sensed a glimmer of that same healing grace in my own heart as I walked with her through that dark valley and back into the sunlight.

Shannon has a message of encouragement and hope so many of us need today. We've all been knocked down and wondered if we had the strength to get back up. As her faith in God's steadfast love deepened, she discovered a resiliency inside herself that she didn't know she possessed.

But Shannon's words aren't just for the deepest sorrows. She is a real person who knows life is always going to throw challenges at us that require a bounce-back spirit. I love her observations and compassion and encouragement—and sense of humor—as she continues to walk the journey of life as a bounce back woman.

One of my favorite stories from the Bible is when Jesus met a woman at the well. (It's all found in John 4.) This woman had lost at love—multiple times. She was shunned by her friends. She was broken by her life experiences. But when she opened herself up to the presence of Jesus, her life was changed forever. In fact, her bounce back was so miraculous, she couldn't help but share the New Life she had found in Jesus. Her faith spilled over and touched the lives of everyone in her village.

I believe that's what Shannon has done for the people in her life. She has shared the healing grace we all need and cherish as bounce back women.

Amy Grant

Note From the Publishers
It's Your Time to Bounce Back!

Have you lost all hope of finding true happiness? Have you given up fighting for your dreams and given in to settling for second best in life? Have you come to believe that healthy relationships are for others—but not you?

Then it's time for you to bounce back! It begins inside your heart and then spills over into your entire life.

The Bounce Back Woman is for you if you are struggling with depression, looking for a way to move past the pain of divorce or another loss, wanting to discover a better future for yourself and your family, or are simply ready to let go and find a way to move on from patterns and situations that hold you back.

Shannon DeGarmo's incredible bounce back story and the lessons she has learned on that journey will provide you with tools to overcome any of life's challenges you are facing today.

KeepTheFaith Publishing is proud to present this new release from Shannon. You can hear more about her story on KeepTheFaith, the #1 nationally syndicated faith based radio program or at keepthefaith.com where you'll find inspirational songs and stories from top recording artists and best selling authors and speakers that are designed to bring you hope.

Your best days are ahead as you look towards the future God has planned especially for you.

Discover Shannon DeGarmo on KeepTheFaith!

Contagious Encouragement at your fingertips, 24/7!

www.KeepTheFaith.com

Part 1

Not The Life I Had Expected

Chapter 1
Anatomy of a Seven-Year Marriage

SEVEN YEARS. IF you live to be one hundred years old, it's only seven percent of your life. Not many of us will make it that long, but you get my point. It's not a whole lot of time. Just a snapshot maybe ... a flash. But, a lot of life can happen in seven years. For me, seven years *was* a lifetime. It was as long as my first marriage lasted. Parts of me became alive in those years. I became a wife and mother. Those are things I had dreamed about. But, other parts of me died. Deceit and betrayal, like a clever cancer, snuck into my marriage and destroyed any part of it that was good. I almost went down with the ship. I hit rock bottom.

We were young when it all started. Isn't that the line that everyone uses? But, we really *were* young. I was 19 years old when I got married. That is only two years older than my daughter right now. How was that even legal? Nevertheless, it doesn't change the fact that I wasn't grown up enough to make a decision that big. But, I fell in love. I totally utterly fell in love with a preacher's son from a Christian rock band. Sounds like the makings of a great county song, doesn't it? It's the truth. He was everything I had ever wanted. He was creative, funny, smart, and on top of everything else, he had a heart for Jesus, and he wanted to share that love through music to those around him. I was raised in the Christian music industry. I was comfortable with it. I knew what a life of touring meant and watched as my mom supported my dad while he was on the road. I had complete understanding and was willing to take it on for my new guy. It was perfect.

We didn't date too long. Now, don't go and get the wrong impression. It wasn't like we dated three weeks or some-thing. We dated six or seven months ... *okay!* We had a small wedding at my parent's house. His dad married us by the fireplace surrounded by just our family. It was a very sweet way to start our life together.

He had a week off from touring. Just long enough for a lit-tle honeymoon, and then off he went on the road. We started our lives. I worked at a Christian record label, and he was off chasing his dream of being in a band and sharing the gospel. We got into a groove pretty quickly. Sometimes I would take off work and travel with him to some of his shows. We stayed in some hotel rooms that didn't have very many stars in their rating and rode around in a van, but we loved it. We were going to look back on these times and call them the *good ole days.* (By the way, I recognize the fact that I haven't used his name, yet. Why you ask? Well, even though I've bounced back, I just have my reasons why I don't want his name in the book. I know some of you can relate.)

~~~~

A couple of years after we were married, I started to get that itch. Y'all know what I'm talking about. When you see babies in the mall and your heart skips a beat, or your arms feel really empty, but you don't know why. *What? Why do I feel this way? Ohhhhh!* I think I want to have a baby. Yes, that is it! Our first little one was born in February. Our daughter, Paisley, was just perfect. I was the ripe old age of 21.

My husband still traveled, but he was making more money by then. So, I was very blessed to be able to quit my job and stay home with her. Now, don't get me wrong. This time was not the easiest. My husband was gone often, and *I* was a baby, who just *had* a baby. I had not the foggiest idea on how to raise a child. I was just so happy that we survived from one day to the next. I really loved being a mom, though, and it seemed like everything was falling into place according to what my expectations of my life were.

Not even two years after our daughter was born, we had a son, Edison. *We didn't waste too much time, I know.* Our daughter was such a source of joy, and then our son joined the club. But, as life does when babies are born, and money gets tight, stress creeps in. We were becoming more financially strapped with the new addition of our son, and the band wasn't earning as much income as we thought it would by that time. So, we had some pretty tough decisions to make. My husband decided he would leave the band and ended up getting a job at a record label in town. Things began to stabilize a bit when that steady income was there.

One day while my babies were taking a nap, I went to the bathroom. We lived in a little one-story house at the time, and the hallway bathroom was the kid's bathroom, as well. I started to put the toys from the tub under the sink when I noticed a folder I hadn't seen before. I opened it to see what it was, and there were magazines in there that would make your hair stand on edge. I had never seen such filth! It was like an outer body experience ... I had squeaky bath toys in one hand and XXX adult magazines in the other. I was totally confused. *Who did this belong to? I know what you're thinking and, yes, denial became very easy for me.*

Since it was before the days when my husband and I had cell phones, I had to wait for my husband to come home from work before I could talk to him about it. It was all I could think about. The kids needed my attention, but I couldn't really focus. *Why was that disgusting stuff in our house?*

Eventually, my husband came home from work. My heart was pounding. I was afraid. I think I knew that this was going to be the first step in my world falling apart. But I bit my tongue as long as I could that evening. I had this terrible thing I wanted to talk to him about, but I couldn't yet because we had two very young children who wanted to spend time with their daddy. So, I tucked this "secret" away in my pocket for a time. I did the mommy and wife stuff. I made dinner, did the dishes, and gave baths. We read stories and sang songs. We did the nightly bedtime kisses and tuck-ins. Finally, the kids were asleep, and I was able to ask my husband about my discovery underneath the bathroom sink.

When I pulled out the teal blue folder from the kitchen where I had stashed it out of the kids reach, my husband didn't look like he had been caught, and he didn't look like he was even nervous. He just kind of laughed and said, "I bet you thought that was mine, didn't you?" I was totally taken aback. Of course I thought it was his! *Wasn't it his?*

"Well, tell me whose it is then."

He then proceeded to tell me that when he was on the road he found it on the stage and grabbed it because he didn't want people thinking it belonged to anybody in the band. He had figured it belonged to one of the kids who came to the concert. When he took it, he shoved the folder into his guitar bag by the stage and forgot about it. Then, he got home; he put his guitar bag away not thinking it was still in there. That was until it fell out when he was leaving for practice one day. But he thought I would be upset upon seeing it. So he threw it under the kids bathroom sink in the hopes he could throw it away when I wasn't around. But he forgot about it.

Then, he got up, took the folder, and threw it in the trashcan.

Hmmmm … I remember thinking: *Why didn't you just tell me about it? Why all this sneaking around?* But the story came out of his mouth so easily, and he didn't even seem shaken that I had found it. So, call it a good heart or denial, I decided to believe my husband. And, I honestly didn't think about it anymore. That's how much I trusted him.

My husband always took care of the bills, which was fine with me. I have never been good with numbers, and I was more than happy to see him take control over that in our marriage. Not too long after the "folder" incident, I was going through the mail and saw a bill I had never before seen. When I opened it, I discovered it was a credit card bill that had thousands of dollars in debt on it, and … it was in my husband's name. Again, my heart just dropped. *Can this be right? Did someone steal his identity and open up a credit card?* Before we had gotten married we had discussed our finances like all new couples are supposed to do. I didn't have any credit card debt, and he said he didn't either. *So, what was this all about?*

I found myself trying to entertain the children while continually thinking about this credit card and the debt on it. My brain was on overload trying to figure out all the different possible scenarios. But, nothing I came up with made any sense ... not even to me. I let the kids crawl all over me; I didn't think they would notice that my mind was totally somewhere else.

When my husband came home and the kids were in bed, I brought out the bill to show him. This time he looked a bit more anxious. He told me that he opened it up in college, and someone stole it and put items on it. However, he was so embarrassed that he didn't tell me about it in the first place. He felt it was best to try to take care of it on his own. He ended by saying he felt ashamed that he wasn't completely honest, but he was trying to pay it off as best as he could. He apologized over and over again. I was so frustrated and angry. I couldn't understand why he would lie in the first place. I asked him why didn't tell me about the card before we got married. Why keep it a secret? And one thing about me is that I totally hate debt! And there we were—thousands of dollars in debt when we could've been working on paying it down all that time. Honestly, his not being upfront hurt my feelings. I felt like he didn't trust me enough to tell me the truth in the first place. What did he think would happen? Did he think I would love him less? Did he think I would have called off the wedding? Even now, I was crazy in love with him, though I felt a pain deep in my heart. He promised he would never do anything like that again. It had been eating away at him, he said. He wanted me to forgive him, which I did. What else could I do? We had been married around five years and had two wonderful children who loved their daddy very much.

I forgave him, but unlike the dirty magazines, this wasn't as easy for me to forget. It gnawed at me. He had kept this secret for *that* long? I asked myself: 'What do I do with this?'

I did the only thing I knew to do: I moved forward.

So, life went on as life does. I thought we would be fine. I was busy after all. With babies, life seemed to be on a perpetual cycle of nap schedules, bottle schedules, and bath time schedules. There were walks to be had and play dates to keep. I had begun songwriting some, and bringing in a teensy weensy bit of income at the time. My husband's record company had closed down, so there we were, again making a job transition. But, this time it was different. My husband had decided to go back to college and finish his degree. Which was totally awesome! Plus, during that time, he had begun to work for my father who owned a small but successful music company. It seemed like things were really beginning to fall into place. We were seeing the stability that an education could offer, and the family business was doing well. My husband had discovered that he really enjoyed the law side of the music business. So, after graduation, he decided to go to law school. It would be a lot more schooling, but my parents decided to foot the bill for him. They wanted to invest in his education so he could then reinvest in the company. It was a 'win-win' situation.

Or so I thought.

Chapter 2
We Need Help

OUR DAYS CONSISTED of pre-school and diapers; and we loved it. I was having a little bit of success in the songwriting world, just a little. But, it helped me contribute to the family financially, which I liked. He was doing great in my dad's company and working hard on law school. We sold our house and were living in an apartment while having a new house built. Life was exciting. It was easy to put doubts and previous hurts aside. Everything seemed to be going pretty well. I was going to have the perfect marriage, family and I life I had always dreamed of after all.

Something totally bizarre did happen to the home we were building (not too interesting of a story, but we couldn't move in there). But even that turned out for the better. We were able to then get a much larger house in the same neighborhood at a discounted rate! Yay for us! I got into painting the kids' rooms. Paisley's was a light purple with dragonflies on the walls, and Edison's was blue with green newts as a border. We even had a small office and a guest room, too! We had never had anything so nice! It was a really great home. But, there was just something about it. I actually remember telling my mom that I didn't think I would be there long. Something inside of me just didn't feel like we belonged. Have you ever had that feeling? You don't know where it comes from, but it's there ... nagging at you. I couldn't explain it at the time other than as a funny feeling.

We moved in late summer and got into the routine pretty quickly. My husband went to work during the days, and law school most afternoons or evenings. I noticed he seemed more distant, but he was basically holding down two jobs. That was understandable. I just thought we had a lot going on. We had two little children that needed lots of attention, and with work and school we didn't see each other much.

As I felt the drift grow wider, I realized we needed some time for just us to reconnect. I asked my in-laws if they could watch the kids for a few days so we could have some grown-up alone time. *You know what I'm talking about?* We just needed some time together to have fun. After we came back from dropping the kids off, I was so excited! We got home late and I ran inside. Couldn't wait to see what we were going to do! No kids. No bedtimes. No rules! As I skipped inside, I looked back at my husband; and he looked like death warmed over. Really ... he had no emotion. He was looking at the floor and wouldn't make eye contact. I was totally confused. We just had a good car ride home. *What's going on?*

We sat on the bed. He asked me if I had ever done something I couldn't take back. *I was like whaaaat? What does that mean?* Well, sure. I've done things I'm not proud of, but whatever it was we could work it out. My husband began talking about his childhood. He was very deep in thought. He began talking about some dark moments from his past. His words didn't all make sense. One thought didn't seem to flow into the next. I asked him if he felt like he needed counseling. Maybe we could go together? Maybe all the stress of work and school was getting to him. He agreed wholeheartedly that it would be good for him to talk to someone. That was a relief. I felt like we were on our way to a solution, even if we didn't have the night I had planned. I really hated to start our weekend off that way, but I thought maybe this was what we needed to do, to get him some help.

We had our weekend. It was not the best. There was a dark cloud hanging over every conversation we had. Everywhere we went. We picked up the kids and began life all over again. But I had no thoughts of giving up on him or us. I loved him and was committed to him. I understood that life isn't perfect. I was particularly pleased we had found a Christian counselor a couple of weeks after that we both really liked. Things began to change immediately—but not for the better.

Chapter 3
Can It Get Worse?

MY HUSBAND STARTED needing extra study sessions at the law school. I knew law school was hard. Soon, he was gone most nights and coming home later and later. When he started working with my father, he got a new amazing thing called a cell phone. I often called to see when he would be home, and soon he stopped picking up my calls. When he came home, he would tell me he had been studying with other students, and I shouldn't call during those times. I asked if we could host the study group at our house. We had more than enough room, and I missed him! Plus, I wanted to meet his friends that he had met at school. I wanted to put faces to names. If I were to be completely honest, there was one particular name I wanted to put a face to … *Erika*. She was a fellow law student who texted my husband often. I don't think it was all about school. When I asked about her, he just said they had become friends. *I am not a jealous person, but there was something about the way he said her name and the expression on his face when he got a text from her that wasn't right.*

I spoke to my husband about it, but he dismissed me as insecure and controlling. *Really? I'm controlling? What is it that you want to do that you don't? You are out every night!*

He also told me that he was dealing with his childhood issues. He began using that line more and more often whenever he felt like I was encroaching on his space, which was almost all the time. He used his mysterious childhood trauma to manipulate all of us. Because, really, how does someone argue with that? However, I just let him fuss at me because his temper was becoming more and more volatile. It was like walking on eggshells when he was around. The kids and I were either too loud, too happy, or too "something" when he was around and it irritated him. He started having outbursts, first at me and then towards the kids. Sad to say, I was happier when he spent more time away.

The counselors were working so hard at trying to figure out what was going on. In fact, they told me that I shouldn't come anymore. They really wanted to spend time with him. *Okay ... sure. Whatever I can do.*

Then, one night he just didn't come home. I called and called. I was thinking that he was in a car accident dead on the side of the road. I didn't know any of the people he was with because he would never let me meet them. He had ensured we were kept quite separate. So I did those things you see people do in the movies. I called the police and the hospitals. I remember thinking: 'This is totally insane. I just can't believe I'm doing this.'

Then, I did something which, unknowingly, would help me immensely. I called my parents and asked for help.

I know that seems like something so small and totally normal. I'm very, very close with my entire family. We are codependent (in a healthy way, I promise!). We all live about ten minutes from each other, but we still go on family vacations together. It's a very sweet relationship. Some of you will be able to relate here: When I was going through such terrible marital times, I didn't want to let anyone know … especially my parents. Not because I didn't trust them, but because I didn't want them to be worried and think badly of my husband. But, I think if I got down to the nitty gritty, I was really ashamed that all this was going on, and *I* wasn't ready to talk about it. Nevertheless, I opened up because I didn't think I had a choice. I was alone with two little kiddos. *I* couldn't go out there and look for him.

By the time the light started coming up, my parents made their way over to the house. My sweet precious little ones woke up completely unaware that I hadn't slept at all, and they were super excited that my parents were at our house. This was when I totally understood the statement: ignorance is bliss. Boy, I would have given anything to be in the dark at that point, too! But, that was a child's dream, and I knew I was a grownup and had to face the tough stuff.

The phone rang. We all looked at each other. Was it the police telling me they had found his car in some ditch? Was it the hospital saying they had his cold, lifeless body in the morgue?

The only way I could find out was to answer the phone. I picked up the receiver, and it was my husband. No apologies, no explanation, no nothing. Just the simple fact that he felt he needed time away to think about his life. Plus, he just didn't feel like coming home. However, he needed a shower and would be home soon. I couldn't even get words out of my mouth before he hung up. *What? You just needed time away?* Everybody needs time away! I needed a vacation from this life, too, but I didn't just go and disappear from the planet!

I looked at my parents and then relayed the information. We were all dumbfounded. But, we decided that we needed to confront the situation immediately. My mom decided to take the kids to breakfast, and my dad and I waited for my husband. It seemed like forever. What felt like 30 minutes was more like two minutes. We didn't know what was going to happen. My husband had been acting so nutso, we didn't have any idea what to expect. I finally heard the sound of the black Toyota coming down the street ... he was home.

We heard the clank of the metal garage door as it opened, then the door to the house. He walked in and stopped when he saw my father and me sitting at the kitchen table. Then, when I thought we were already at an all-time family low ... it got lower.

My husband immediately copped a bad attitude. He was quite irritated that my dad was there, and acted like he couldn't understand why I had overreacted and called him. It was like a switch went off. My dad stood up and got in my husband's face; and then my husband got in my dad's face. I swear I thought they were going to start punching each other. My heart was breaking right then and there. The situation was bad enough already, but then to have the two men I loved the most fighting was just about all I could take.

My dad was trying to put the fear of God in my husband demanding that he not do that to us again. My husband was not to disappear because he needed time to himself. This was not to turn into a habit, and the rest of us weren't going to live our lives worried about his whereabouts. My husband was still acting like it wasn't a big deal, but finally gave us the promise that we wanted. He promised that he would not spend another full night away from home; he would never be gone all night long again. Funny how he worded that promise ... *ALL* night long.

Chapter 4
Yes, It Can

HE NEVER WAS gone again ALL night long. But, he started coming home anytime between three and five o'clock in the morning. I guess he considered that as keeping his promise. I didn't know where he was or whom he was with. I often stayed up wringing my hands and pacing. I would wait upstairs in that office straining my ears to hear a car, or I stared out the window to see the glare of lights pulling into the driveway. When he finally would come home, I would run downstairs and hop into the bed pretending to be asleep so I wouldn't give him the gratification of knowing I had stayed up all night thinking about him. Then, he would sleep for about two hours and wake up and go to work, or ironically, go to counseling. This was our routine for five or six terrible, heartbreaking months. Through it all, I kept up the façade with the children that all was well. But, all along, I was killing myself trying to maintain normalcy in a totally abnormal situation. That was the saddest part, really. The normal was stripped away bits at a time, and replaced by a warped, sick, abusive life, which I was beginning to lose myself in. It was like I was on robotic autopilot. I was raising the kids in the best way I could (under the circumstances), at the same time I was pushing all the issues away. It was not like I didn't want to face reality. I didn't know what do to with it all. I didn't have any solutions.

He would come home after work and stay for about an hour. Then, off again to who knew where. One night, I tried to catch him on his way out. I was putting the kids to bed and I heard him getting his stuff together to leave. I rushed downstairs and caught him at the door. I just wanted to know what was so bad at home that he felt the need to leave all the time. What was it about *me* that made him leave? I was searching for an answer ... *any* answer. He turned around to me, looked me straight in the eyes, and said that he didn't think I had a lot to offer him. He continued by saying that the only think endearing about me was my smile, but that had lost its luster as well. I think my mouth just hung open. No words came out. I was stunned. It wasn't the first time he had said terrible things to me, but it was the first time I began to feel all this had nothing to do with me. *Really? You leave because I have nothing to offer you?* I didn't have the answers about what was going on, but I did know that the statement he gave me was a selfish, self-centered arrogant answer. And no matter what I had to offer it would never be enough.

A couple of days later, it was a Friday. He came home for his normal hour after work, but this time was different. He got out a suitcase and started packing. When I asked where he was going, he said he was going camping. *Camping?* We had been married for almost seven years, and we had NEVER been camping. We didn't even own a tent! When I asked who he was going camping with, he told me that it was his friends, and I didn't need to know who they were. Well, this was it. I was so tired of all the bull! It had been building up inside me for months. I was tired of being pushed aside, not listened to, feeling unworthy, emotionally abused and ignored ... and it all came out that Friday afternoon. I let him know exactly what I thought he was doing with his 'so called' friends. I told him if he went camping, things would not be the same when he returned. My head hurt because I was yelling so much. I couldn't catch my breath as the tears dripped off my chin. I didn't know how things would be different when he got back, but I knew they would.

The kids were upstairs in their rooms and easily overheard my outburst. I had been trying so hard to keep the house 'normal,' but I couldn't keep up the pretense any longer. I had to release these terrible feelings, and really, I had to stick up for myself. What was happening wasn't okay. It had to be said. I was tired of being a doormat. I needed to feel worthy again. I could not keep my family together by myself ... no matter how hard I tried.

He watched me as I waved my arms and carried on with all of my threats. He sat there on the floor with his suitcase and bags around him. He didn't respond with any words. He just giggled. He laughed at me. I thought this man had lost all attachment with reality. Our marriage was falling apart and he was laughing? He finished packing, stood up, said he would be back on Sunday, and closed the front door. He didn't even look back. Here I was: A scrawny, emotionally beaten wife that has just released months of frustration only to be responded to with laughter.

As I heard his car drive away, I sat on the floor and cried. Not only was I the verbal punching bag, now I was being ignored. And, honestly, being ignored felt worse than being yelled at. It was like I didn't even *exist*. I was at a crossroads. On one hand, I was in a terrible marriage. I knew my husband was doing things he shouldn't, and I wanted to get far, far away. On the other hand, I had such faith in Jesus; I thought for sure he could heal whatever was ailing us. And I believe that divorce is wrong. I could not leave and divorce my husband because he was mean. There were too many unanswered questions...too many unknowns. As I sat there on the floor with no direction, I looked to God. I told him, plain as day, that I just couldn't go on like this anymore. Something had to change. I simply asked the Lord to either end it or fix it. I didn't care what the answer was. I didn't care what it would take. No more being in this muddy no man's land. I *needed* to have resolution.

It's funny how God knows what you need exactly when you need it. He knows when you are truly done, and when He needs to intervene.

Chapter 5
Computer Miracles

THE VERY NEXT day, while the kids took their naps, I walked up the stairs into the office. We had gotten a pink mac (*Y'all remember those? Some of the first apple computers, which came in all the colors?*) I had decided to check to see if we had this new thing called 'online banking.' I had overheard someone talking about it, and I wanted to check it out. This was just one hint of how I was *NOT* involved in the finances. I didn't even know if we banked online. (*Just a little tad of advice: be involved.*) I had no idea why I was interested on that particular day, but I was. Anyway, I sat down and typed in the website. Automatically, without any password, our account came up. Well, at least I thought it was *our* account until I started seeing the different transactions that were posted. This was not the mundane account that I knew we had where the most exciting transaction was Target or McDonalds. No, on this account there were transactions where he had paid hundreds of dollars for restaurants, flowers, and liquor. Some of the restaurant bills were over $300.00. He had ordered flowers for someone, and the cost was over $400.00. And I knew I hadn't gotten as much as a weed from my husband in a long time. My eyes couldn't even process all that I was seeing. The blood was rushing to all different parts of my body. My breath was quickening. I was actually looking at something that could give me a glimpse into what was going on. But, I was still so confused. The deposits and withdrawals on this account were thousands of dollars. *Where was the money coming from?* But I did know one thing. I knew, without a shadow of a doubt, I was looking at a miracle. I knew it was God's way of answering my prayer. He wasn't going to allow me to be the fool anymore, and although it was hard to look at, I was so grateful. Finally, I had something … some kind of starting point.

I decided to call my husband. He didn't pick up … *no surprise there*! I left him a message that he needed to call back immediately, that there had been an emergency. Well, I guess that sparked his curiosity because he called back within ten minutes. I could hear laughter in the background when he asked me about the emergency. All I said was four little words: *I found your account.* Silence. He said nothing. I could still hear the background noise, so I knew we hadn't been disconnected. And then I said, *"You need to come home."* That was it. The only word he said was *"Okay."* I didn't know what that meant. Was he coming home within the hour? Was he coming home tonight or tomorrow? I had no idea.

About an hour later he called and said he would be home in about two hours. This time, the man who had laughed at me the day before during my heart wrenching moment, sounded nervous.

While I still had him on the phone, I asked the basic questions: *What is this account? Where did all this money come from? Who are you spending it on??* He then told me, in about a handful of sentences, he had developed a cocaine habit, and that he had taken about $10,000 from my parents to support it. Then, still with a straight voice, he said the flowers were for me, but then he had decided I didn't deserve them. And, for whatever reason, he had thrown them away.

Oh My Gosh. I heard all of the words, but it took a long time for them to settle into my brain. But, out of all of that ... what hurt the worst was that he had stolen from my family. My family had taken in my husband. They had loved him, supported him, and adopted him as their own. And as he sat around their dinner table and prayed for blessings, he was stealing from them. I was shattered in a million pieces. I asked myself: 'Who am I talking to?' I didn't even know my own *husband.*

So, I hung up the phone and called my steadfast parents. Reluctantly, but thankfully, I let them into my sick and twisted world. So, again, we did the tag team thing. My dad waited with me as I waited for this perfect stranger I called my husband. In the meantime, I called my husband's parents and told them the whole story. I told them about the entire year, how terrible it had been. How he told me that he had a drug problem. How I didn't feel safe with him around. I felt totally psycho telling my husband's father all of this. But, I had a goal in mind, too. I didn't want my husband in the house. I already knew he was unstable emotionally and a liar, but now we were throwing in a drug addiction and stealing. I knew there was no way I was going to allow him to stay around the children in that kind of condition. I wanted my father-in-law to come and get him. I knew the trip was about six hours, but this was one of those life-changing events. He finally agreed to come and pick him up. It just needed to happen.

All that time, my husband had been telling me it was my fault he had been doing these terrible things. He was blaming me for all of his issues. At that time, I knew I still didn't know the whole truth, but what I did know helped me let go of a lot of that blame. I knew I had been pushing the lies away like pesky flies. But I finally felt like I was beginning to have a glimpse of what was really going on.

So we waited.

Chapter 6
A Perfect Storm

IT SEEMED TO take forever for my husband to get home. My father and I discussed what we were going to say. We tried to think of all the different ways this could play out. There we were. We were victims of stealing, addiction and lies. We had been handed a terrible mess not of our making, and we had been handed the broom and dustpan, too. Totally unfair, but totally life.

I curled up on my oversized purple chair, and my dad sat on the couch. His face showed both pity and concern. I'm sure he thought I would have a nervous breakdown at any moment. He looked as if he thought I would start pulling out my hair and throwing things from the shelves. I'd lost so much weight living in complete chaos, and I looked skinny and weak, and I was broken hearted, too.

Where was God during all of this? Well, I've come to learn that the times when we can't see God's hand in things are the times when He's not leading us, but carrying us.

My husband finally came home. He walked in and found us there. I didn't get up because, honestly, seeing him made me physically sick. He sat on the couch; there was nothing but silence. It was awkward in a billion different ways. Who would speak first? Well, I knew for sure it would not be me.

My dad started. He was using his intimidating dad voice, the voice parents use when you are afraid to look at them, but also afraid not to. That was the voice. My father meant business, and I was letting him talk. My brain was total mush, and I felt like my bones were made of Jell-O.

So, here is the long and short of the conversation:

Dad: What happened?

Husband: (same old story) I took around $10,000 to support a drug habit. But, I'm going to pay it all back.

Dad: Is that all?

Husband: Yes, that is all.

Dad: (getting a little closer to my husband's face and using a deeper growl; it didn't even sound like a voice) Is that all?

Husband: Well, I think I took more like $15,000. But, I promise I'm going to pay it all back.

Dad: (knowing the story had started changing, he figured there must be more) Oh, I see. You've taken a bit more. How long has this been going on? Is there another woman in the picture?

Husband: (looking wounded that my father would even ask such a question) I've been stealing for about a year. Of course not. I would never do that to Shannon.

Dad: So, that's it. You've stolen $15,000 from me, and it's been going on for about a year. And you are not seeing anyone else. That better be the truth. If it's not, I'm going to find out. I'll hire whoever I need to so we can figure this out.

Husband: (looking a little more unsettled than before) Well, I may have taken more like $30,000, and it may have been happening for more than a year. And there is someone else, but she's totally just a friend ... a very close friend. Our relationship could be considered inappropriate.

Ummmm ... what the heck was that supposed to mean, I thought. Of course, for the very first time, I was seeing my husband for what he was. It was like looking at someone I had never seen before. His face even looked different. He was staring straight into our eyes and still lying. He was on the verge of losing everything, and he was still living in LaLa Land. I truly thought I would hurl, faint, or freak out. Maybe, I thought, I should do all three at the same time.

My dad and I exchanged glances. But, before we could say anything, my father-in-law arrived. It was surreal to see everyone in such out of context circumstances. Normally when we visited with my father-in-law we would all be excited. But, no one was feeling anywhere close to that.

My husband wondered out loud why his dad was at our house, and I explained that I didn't want him to stay. He looked at me with complete shock and said, "So I don't have a say if I can stay or not?" I told him, *no*. He got very irate; he stood and paced the floor. He told us we couldn't make him leave; he could do what he wanted. *And, I guess part of that was true. I wondered how I could make him leave. I knew I couldn't pick him up and take him out.* So, we told him if he stayed, we would call the police. That scared him enough to settle down.

My dad and I explained as much as we could to my father-in-law. All the while, my husband sat on the couch in complete disbelief; he could not understand why I didn't want him in the house. I thought he was really upset because he had to go with his father. I don't think he wanted to stay in the house with us; I just don't think he wanted to leave town.

As they packed up to leave for a few days, my father-in-law asked, "What are you going to do about this?" I let the question sink in. *What am I going to do about this?* I knew I could not make any decisions yet because I was dealing with someone who lied, and I didn't know the whole story.

I also knew I loved my family, and I didn't want to get a divorce. I thought I would do anything I could to keep it together. But, I also knew, it was not all up to me. I told my father-in-law that I didn't know what I was going to do, and I truly meant it.

My husband became very angry as he was leaving. When he was putting his stuff into my father-in-law's car, he stopped by his own car and opened his trunk. He started pulling out boxes and boxes of stuff. *What was all that?* He also started to pack his laptop ... the laptop that my dad had bought for him to use for the company. It was not my husband's, but the property of the company. It held all the records of what he was involved in for the company. Plus, my husband seemed incredibly attached to it. We decided he shouldn't take it. It didn't belong to him, and it likely held answers to some of our issues. But, my husband managed to wiggle his way through it. He said he wasn't going to be able to do his homework for school if he didn't have it. So, we reluctantly let him take it with the promise that he wouldn't use it unless he was with my father-in-law. Plus, he had to get whatever homework he needed off of it and send it back to us. He wasn't too happy about that either.

As they drove off, I felt the need to go upstairs and peek in on my children. Did they hear anything that just went on? I needed to see them. When I looked into their rooms, my heart nearly broke. All I could see were their little heads nestled in their pillows. All I wanted to do was protect them from the crap wave that was coming towards them. I knew I wasn't going to be able to shield them from everything, but I promised I would do whatever it took to honor them as we all walked through the mud ... together.

Chapter 7
Peeling Back The Onion

THAT NIGHT, I slept better than I had in a year. I know that probably sounds totally crazy, but I was no longer worrying about where my husband was or whom he was with. I knew where he was, and it wasn't my job to babysit him. I woke up to little feet hitting the floor upstairs. It didn't take long for one pair of feet to turn into two pairs, and then they bounded down the stairs to get in my bed. It was so nice to be rested! I was awake before they got there, and had the warm covers all ready for them to get into so we could start our day huddled together. They came to the doorway with their wacked out hair and their swollen eyes. Paisley had her binky in her hand and Eddie had his bear. They came full force with all their energy hurling towards the bed. I separated myself for a moment and thought, 'This will be it. I am looking at the final seconds of my children's lives when things are *normal*. When they don't have to think about the bad that is in the world. When they don't have to worry about what will happen to mommy and daddy. It's the last I will see of their little faces carrying the purest form of innocence.

It didn't take long for Paisley to wonder where her daddy was. She knew he should've been coming back soon. But, I remembered the promise I made the night before about honoring them, and this was the best way to do it ... to be honest. Honor them with truth (but truth on their level). This is how it went:

Paisley: Where is Daddy?

Me: Daddy went to Grandma and Grandpa's house in Kentucky (which he did).

Paisley: Why?

Me: Daddy and I had a long talk last night, and we thought it would be best if he went up there to visit for a little while.

Paisley: Why?

Me: Because Daddy did some things that he should not have done, and he needs to go and be with his parents to think for a little bit.

Paisley: What did he do?

Me: He broke a promise that he made to me when we got married. Now, he has to go and think about what he did.

Paisley: Oh...can I have breakfast now?

It was pretty straightforward and simple. Not too flashy, but real. Eddie was not even interested. He was only two years old. His main concern at the moment was working the remote control to get SpongeBob on the television.

My parents called shortly after breakfast. I could hear the worry in my mother's voice. However, I think she was surprised when I told her I slept so well. I guess I was just wiped out. It's amazing what a good night's sleep can do for you! I asked her what I should do next? It was such a huge question. None of us knew what to do. I knew I wasn't the first person in the world to go through something like this, but I was only 26 years old. Most of my friends weren't even married, let alone already going through really tough times. My parents said they knew of a crisis counselor that might help guide me. I took the first available appointment I could get.

My mom asked if I had ever seen any bank statements from the other account that I didn't know about. Gosh! I never even thought of that! We weren't just dealing with a cheating addict husband, but we were also dealing with a crime that had been committed against my parents. I had never seen any statements. I didn't know where they were. My mom suggested I call the local post office to see if my husband had a P.O. box because statements could have been sent to one. A P.O. box? I thought. What? That's craziness.

Who would open a P.O. box for bank statements? That would mean he had really thought this whole thing out.

I called the post office and asked if there was a postal box in my husband's name. I gave them all of his information. The woman who had answered then kind of giggled and said that it was ironic because he had just called and cancelled the box not ten minutes earlier. I could not believe it. I then asked her how long ago he had opened it, and she said she couldn't remember exactly, but knew it was a few years at least. I really think my eyes rolled back into my brain. This is when it began …the wrinkle between my eyebrows. My eyebrows had that look of total confusion for about two years, and then the wrinkle just stuck. It was born during that time. It's just one of the many things that I took away from that era.

I then decided to call my husband. He picked up the phone. Wow, this was twice in two days that he answered my phone call! We were on a roll (insert sarcasm here). We were both silent for about 30 seconds, but it seemed like forever. Then I asked him how he was doing. Isn't that sicko? Me, the one who had been railroaded, asking *him* how he was doing. He said he was a little tired from the trip, but he was fine. *Oh, that's good.* He then started to tell me all about what he was going to do while he was up there. He was planning on seeing some old friends and seeing a movie. *Oh … My … Gosh … for real? The world is falling apart around us, and you are going to go see a movie.* It was becoming glaringly clear that he was in denial. Not one question about me or the kids ... just all about his life. I had never known what a narcissistic personality was before, but I was getting a crash course in it. I then asked him about the P.O. box. Without even pausing to take a breath, he said, "What P.O. box?" *So, we are going to play this game, I thought.* I remind him about the P.O. box that he had just cancelled that morning ... the one that he had for the last few years. The one that the lady in the post office had just told me about! My voice was getting more and more stressed. Finally, he admitted he had one after I made it impossible for him not to. But, he lied about how long he had had it, and he also said it was just a coincidence that he had canceled it that day. He was going to cancel it regardless ... *yeah, right.*

I hung up the phone. By that time I knew I was dealing with someone who did not know lies from reality. How was I going to go through this with someone who was so far into a world he created that he couldn't see his way out? Jesus, I thought, only You can fix this.

I saw the counselor who told me I should think about taking the kids to see their grandparents and their dad. Looking back, I don't know if that was the best advice. But, I was very stressed, and I was taking any kind of advice given, as long as it didn't sound insane.

Chapter 8
A Little Trip

AFTER SEVERAL DAYS, I took the kids to see him. I was only going to stay for a night and leave the next day. My husband acted like he hadn't seen the kids in five years. He had been gone every night the past several months. He hadn't done one goodnight kiss or bath time since I could remember, but for some reason that day he acted like he had been away at war and had just come home for a family reunion.

It was the weirdest visit ever. My husband was acting like nothing was going on. He played with the kids after dinner. When we put the kids to bed, I sat down with everyone. We all were just looking at each other. It was almost like we had too much to say, so we couldn't say anything. Does that make any sense?

After the kids went to bed my husband and I talked. I felt like I needed some kind of direction from him as to where all this was going. *Did he want to try to work it out? Was he sorry?* I decided it would be best to talk about what I was willing to do. I couldn't control him and his actions, but I could control mine. I told him that even after all of this I was still willing to work it out. In time, I could forgive. In time, we could heal. When I said, "I do," I meant it ... forever. I also knew that it would take years of hard work to get through something like that. But, I was willing to do it for him ... me ... us and ours.

After I gave him my emotional *schpiel*, he looked directly at me and said, "How do I know that after all this work, that I still won't be unhappy with you? It's just not something I want to do." And, there you have it. He also told me that he had been researching divorce, and I should file because he was the one that messed up. He said he would be fine with that. My head was spinning. It was like he was talking about a pair of shoes or a meal he didn't want. But, it was three hearts he was trading in. And, for what? Only he could answer the question.

I had my answer, and I decided to go to bed in one of the guest rooms upstairs. I looked at my feet going up the brown shag carpeting and thought to myself, 'I just cannot believe this is happening. I'm going to be a divorcée. I'm going to be a single mom.' Try to let something like that sink in ... it was something I had never even ventured to think about.

My husband stayed in his childhood room downstairs, which was more than fine with me. While I was getting ready for bed, my parents called. It was one of those conversations that I knew wasn't going to be good from the second I picked up the phone. Remember that laptop that was taken. Well, UPS finally delivered it to my parents. They had taken it to a computer guru. Both of them got on the phone and told me that it didn't look good. He had downloaded a program that would burn the hard drive, so whoever was looking through it wouldn't be able to see the history. So much for the promise that he wouldn't use it without his dad being there. But, computers always have a way of keeping track of everything. They had found two sets of financial books. One was the real financials for the company, and the other was a fake set that my husband had kept to keep my dad in the dark about what he was doing. If that wasn't bad enough, they were able to access all of the websites he had been viewing. And those titles suggested any wife and mother's worst nightmare. My husband had been accessing pure evil on the internet. The images he had been looking at were spiritually damaging and mind killing. He had allowed it to infiltrate our home and his heart. My mind became a complete hurricane of feeling. It seemed like every day that passed got more and more terrible. Every time the phone rang, I was afraid to answer it because it was ALWAYS bad news. This situation was like peeling back an onion, there was just more layers. I began to understand why people lived in denial ... it was a much easier place to live because reality sucked.

I felt the need to scoop up my kids and get the heck out of there. First thing in the morning, we packed up and went back home. But the place that housed our furniture and our belongings ... it didn't feel too much like home anymore. I sat there thinking about all these problems:

1. I was married to a drug addict who had a girlfriend and a very nasty computer habit, which I had no idea how to address.

2. I had a stack of bills, which were collecting dust because I didn't have the money to pay them.

3. I had no prospect of a job that could even come close to paying those bills because I only had a high school diploma.

Needless to say, this was a very bad time in my life. I was beaten down. I was so ashamed of my husband and his choices. Not only did he betray me and my family, he had reached a level of such depravity that it was incomprehensible. I couldn't grasp that I had to even think something like this could happen. *Am I an idiot? How could I not know?* I felt like a zero, zilch, a nothing.

Chapter 9
I Need A Plan

I WAS CERTAIN about one thing, though: I was not going to allow all this sin, all this chaos to prevent me from making the best choices for my children. Trust me, I didn't want to talk about the fact that my husband had a girl on the side, or that he was looking at porn on the computer. As a wife and as a woman, it tore at the very foundation of womanhood. The whispers that said we were not beautiful enough or desirable enough, that our husbands had to go elsewhere to be satisfied. Although I wanted to tuck all that information under a rock and let it rot because it made me feel so awful, I knew that wouldn't be the best thing for my kids. But I also knew I couldn't let them be around a man who was in such a dark place. I didn't care if they had shared DNA, I would never place them in a position where they might be unsafe. I could never have lived with myself if I had buried my head in the sand and looked the other way. So, I did what I had to do.

I knew he had all kinds of activity on his laptop, but the "burn" program that he had put on it ruined many of the files. Next I tried the pink mac. I went to the history. Well, oh well ... it was as bad as I thought. I hit the print button. I did my best not to stare at the screen because some of the images were just too much to look at. I kept my eyes on the keyboard. Some of the websites were password protected, and I don't know how I did it, but I guessed some of them correctly. I hit print again. In less than one hour, I had a huge folder filled with the underbelly of society. My heart broke for myself, my family, and for all those faces that were on the screen in front of me. I had no coping mechanisms for this kind of stuff. It was too much. I just cried.

Not too long after that afternoon, I met with a lawyer. I wanted a very, very good one. I knew they were expensive, so I asked my parents to front me the money. I promised to pay them back when I sold my house (*yeah...my parents paid for my divorce. Sounds like another country song*). But, it really was the best decision. I knew what I wanted, and that was to make sure the children were safe. Plus, I wanted to be able to keep my husband accountable for any future choices. As I sat in my lawyer's office, I just couldn't believe I was really there. It felt like I was hovering above looking down on the scene. I told him I didn't want the children to be in my husband's care unless he was healthy. I was scared to death, and he saw it. I showed him the file I had created, and his eyebrows went up. He explained to me that the folder contained evidence of a horrible addiction, and that many of the sites could be deemed illegal, as well. I had already guessed as much because, although I had tried not to, I did see some of the pictures on the screen while printing. But sometimes we just need someone else to tell us the truth when we are in rough situations. If self-preservation had not kicked in, I might have continued to live in denial. But, this was too important. I knew it was something that had to be addressed. The lawyer asked if my husband and I would be willing to go to a mediator to discuss our plans for the children. The mediator was special because he was a child psychologist, as well, and would have the children's best interests at heart.

My husband was more than happy to go. So, we went. We talked about everything from Christmas, to weekends, and even weeks in the summer. It was like talking about a rental house, not real living breathing children. It was crushing. This was their lives we were talking about. After we created a skeletal schedule, the psychologist asked my husband if he would be willing to go to a behavioral testing clinic. He thought my husband should be evaluated to ensure he was suitable to be alone with the children. Of course, my husband said. He said all that computer stuff had occurred when he was a totally different person. He assured the psychologist and me that it was all going to turn out just fine. Well ... it did turn out fine, but not in the way my husband thought. He did not fare well, and the clinic suggested supervised visitation until certain therapies had taken place. In addition, he would have to submit to a lie detector test every six months until the children were 18-years-old to ensure that my husband hadn't gone back to his old habits.

Oh my gosh! Oh my gosh! I couldn't believe it. I was so relieved. I finally knew I wouldn't have to stay awake worrying that they would be put in compromising situations by their father or by any of his friends. I didn't have to worry about their safety. It was an answer to prayer. But I was also so sad we had reached this place. I had to be the one to ensure that my children's father would not harm them. I don't think a word has been created to describe that feeling. I became a single momma. I did not have every other weekend, or some nights off. I didn't have the weeks in the summer or extra help. But I was fine with that. I wouldn't have traded it for anything. I was happy to be the one with them. It was an honor.

Chapter 10
What Happens Next?

ONCE I KNEW my children would be safe and the divorce was underway, I still had money problems. Yep, those darn bill collectors can get really serious when they want their money! My now *ex-husband* was not the best at paying child support. I couldn't depend on him. My parents were gracious enough to float me while I tried to get a plan together. But I knew that couldn't last forever. I needed a plan. I couldn't afford to keep my house, so we had to sell it. *But, where to go after that?* I knew I needed an education. My lack of job qualifications and education meant I would be looking at very low wages. I would need to work two jobs. *When would I ever see my kids?* They had already experienced so much change. They had lost their dad. I didn't want them to lose me to a couple of jobs that I didn't even like.

I knew I had no choice; I went back to school. I looked into family housing, but it meant we would have to leave my

support system (*and single moms NEED a support system*).
We already had gone through so much; I didn't want to
take the kids away from their pre-school and friends. So, I
took my parents up on a very generous offer: to live with
them while I went to school to get my teaching degree. *And
that, my friends, is a whole other story!*

Within six months I had discovered my husband was a total
stranger, and I was living in a true made for T.V. Lifetime
Network movie. I had sold my house, moved in with my
parents, divorced my husband, became a single mom, and
started school. Can you say *stressful?* Can you say *nervous
breakdown?*

During this time, I truly leaned into Jesus. I really didn't
have any choice. The waves of life kept battering me, but
Jesus kept picking me up. The only thing in my control was
the method in which I would handle the emotional blows
that were headed my way. Each time I got comfortable,
something else would come into play, and I had to learn
how to incorporate the new into the old. It continued that
way for about a year-and-a-half, while I continued to
navigate and guide my sweet children's hearts as they
yearned for consistency and love. Their little lives had been
turned topsy-turvy. I knew those little ones prayed that I
would hold it all together for them. What they didn't know
was that I was praying for the same thing.

~~~~

Since my husband could only see the children supervised, I was the first in line to supervise. *Oh my goodness.* Talk about hard! Thankfully he didn't ask to see the kids too often, so I didn't have to put myself in that position too much. But, occasionally we all went to the park or out to eat. I had to go to his apartment sporadically. Each time I had to pray my way through the awkwardness. I knew on the surface, people would look at us and think, *Oh, look at that happy family. What a beautiful thing to see.* And, all the while, I was thinking: This experience is worse than a root canal without any anesthesia. Each experience was painful and nauseating. The kids clung to his every word and laughed at all his jokes. While I watched, I always thought: He gets these precious visits from these tiny angels. He gets the smiles and the love, but he doesn't have to put forth any investment. He doesn't have to sacrifice anything. He's got it so easy. But, as I continued to work through the forgiveness process with him, I realized it was the life 'stuff' that makes it all worth it. It was the hard things that were bringing the children and me together. I knew I would rather have the years of raising those two children by myself than the seconds of smiles and laughter any day. He was really missing out.

Even though my divorce had been finalized, the problems still weren't over. We still had the issue of the stolen money and the way he did it. He had claimed stealing $30,000, but that was not even close. It turned out he had stolen upwards of $80,000, and he had forged checks to do it, which is a felony ... a really BIG no-no. Not only had he

forged checks, but when I sold the house and started going
through our personal paperwork, I discovered he had
mortgaged our home, as well. Just one thing after another.
No one could say the man didn't know how to spend
money!

My ex-husband had resumed his life. He was working at a
law firm, hanging out with friends, and acting like none of
this had ever happened or even mattered. We continually
caught him in lies. We couldn't trust a word that passed
through his lips. It was as if he thought because he had
fooled us for so long, we were surely brainless. He was
neither repentant nor broken. There was only arrogance and
vile behavior.

One day, my parents approached me about the stolen
money. They were deciding if they would take the case to
the district attorney. Plus, the bank wanted their money
back and was willing to do whatever it took. My parents
asked how I felt about it. Would I be supportive of them
pressing charges? I think they needed to know if that would
be the straw that broke the camel's back. I had known this
conversation was coming, and I felt different ways about it.
On one hand, the kids already had experienced so much
adjustment. They had suffered enough. On the other hand,
there is something to be said for accountability and
consequence. We learn so much from our mistakes, but we
don't learn anything if we are not held accountable for our
choices. Honestly, that's what did it for me. How could I
raise my children to respect authority, the law, and others

around them if their own dad wasn't held to the same standard? *Plus, he was still in law school!* The man who wrote bad checks for years was really a criminal pretending to be someone *upholding* the law. It didn't sit well with me.

About a year after the charges were filed, I received a phone call from my ex-husband. He was pretty upset. After all, he had been arrested at the law firm where he worked, and in front of his co-workers. That *was* pretty bad. I just sat and listened. I had become better at putting up boundaries with him. Supervising the visitation with the children had helped. Listening to him, I felt bad. I honestly did. Life was about to get really hard for him. But, I never regretted my choice; I supported the bank in pursuing him. I knew in my gut it was the best thing.

He was sentenced to eight years in jail. He served several months, and the rest was on probation. I never took the children to the jail to visit him. I didn't want that to be a memory for my children. It would totally scare them to see their dad in jail. After he was sentenced, I told him he could call collect whenever he wanted. Plus, he could write whenever he wanted, too. I promised I would read the letters to the children and keep them for him. I kept my promise. He only wrote about four or five letters during that time. Not too long ago my daughter wanted to see those letters again. They are hers now.

Chapter 11
Forgiveness

ABOUT A YEAR after we got divorced, I knew I was going to have to let all the junk go. I knew the Lord was knocking on my heart, and I was going to have to forgive my ex-husband. It was a struggle. Everything was. Nothing was easy. My life had been turned upside down, sideways, down ways and every which way because of that man. I had questioned my worth, my sanity, my purpose, and my Creator because of his actions. I had nightmares about him coming into my home and killing me. I would wake up in pools of sweat and complete anxiety. I had been to the threshold of hell with two children because of sin's consequences. I had been tossed aside, deemed not "enough." My children had been crushed and humiliated. Their tears only fueled my anger. Their questions only made me hate him more. But, Jesus knew I couldn't be the mom I wanted to be if I was bitter and angry. He knew I couldn't lift my hands to Him if I was carrying so much baggage. So, tap … tap, He went. In the still of the night,

He would whisper what He did *for* me was bigger than what my husband did *to* me. Tap-tap again. The Lord would allow me to see glimpses of what life could be without all this anger. For instance, one day, I just totally forgot to think about what happened. For a year, my ex-husband had been the topic of so many conversations and issues. But, for one day, the Lord gave me a gift of not allowing him into my thoughts. That night, I recognized how great of a day it was. How I was not on that rollercoaster of emotions. It was a boring and magnificent day! Is this what it will be like after forgiveness? No more anger. No more distrust. No more victim-like mentality?

~~~~

One night I was in bed reading my Bible, and I just knew it was the time. God knows the perfect timing in things, and this was it. But, I was still holding on to the anger for some reason. I prayed to Jesus, "I forgive him. Now I can move on." It was a weak prayer that meant nothing. Have you ever had those? You pray, but you know your heart is not in it. Praying just because you know it's the right thing to do. I was going through the typical Christian motions. And I didn't feel anything different. I wanted it to feel supernatural. Instead, it just felt blah.

One thing about our Jesus is that He truly loves an authentic heart. I am so happy He called me out on my ridiculous fake prayer. I knew my prayer was insincere. The Lord told me to try again.

So, I did. But, this time I wasn't praying inside my mind. I sat up and looked to the Heavens. I said, "Lord, I forgive him. Take all the hatred, anxiety, stress, and anger away. I don't want to live this way. I'm done." Y'all, I'm not trying to sound mystical, but I truly did feel a weight lift from my shoulders. It was as if a heavy coat was taken off my body. I physically felt myself straighten up and breathe easier. I felt no more anger and bitterness about things from the past. I felt peace. The Lord's promises are so true. I'm living proof of that. It seemed like such a small thing to do, but it was not. It was huge. I was so thankful to let it all go.

But the Lord wasn't going to be completely satisfied with that. It's one thing to forgive someone, but we are also called upon to love everyone. *Ummm ... but I don't think my situation is the same. I really don't think this counts for me.* Yeah, it totally counted. *What the heck?? It bothers me that my ex-husband and I live in the same country! How can I love this guy after what he did?* I knew that I was called to pray for him. It really is one of the most loving things you can do for a person. Pure, honest, heartfelt prayer. So, I did.

I didn't want to pray for him, and, at first, I couldn't get the words out because I couldn't think of anything to pray for. I realized I was going to have to make it a habit. I had to start praying even if I didn't have the right words to say.

My first prayer was simple: *Lord, if my ex-husband gets hit by a semi-truck I would be okay with that.* No judgment please! I didn't *ask* for him to get run over, I just said *if* it happened I would be okay with it. I know, I know, it's not the best prayer, but it was the only one I could find to get me started. I moved on to better prayers eventually. However, I did notice when I began to pray for him, my cold heart started to warm up again. I had become so robotic for so long just in order to survive; I had neglected my humanity, the parts that were vulnerable and innocent. They were coming alive within me once again. Jesus truly knows what we need, doesn't He?

I realized I needed to tell my ex-husband that I forgave him. That was part of the whole deal. I called him. This was a very rare occasion. I *never* called him. When he picked up I was so nervous. Telling him meant that I could never be mad about this 'stuff' again. It meant I couldn't hold it over his head anymore. It meant it was over. Honestly, it was a bit hard to let it all go. But, it had to be done. The words just spilled out, *I forgive you.* I think I was expecting an overwhelming response about how I had just changed his life; but that didn't happen. He just said, "Thank you." And that was that. I was free.

Now, don't get me wrong. Forgiveness did not mean that all was forgotten. I still lived by the parenting plan that was in place. I didn't invite him over for dinner, and we didn't have long talks at night. We did not become best friends. It would not have been healthy for me. I had been manipulated for so long; I had to keep a safe distance. But, I hoped for his happiness and that he knew how valued he was by Jesus. I hoped he knew about second chances and that Christ had died for every single one of us. Forgiveness doesn't mean you never get upset anymore. I just couldn't get upset about the stuff I had forgiven him for. He'd done other things over the years, and I forgave him for that, too. I was sure he'd forgiven me, as well, as we navigated life post-divorce. It was an ongoing process. People are all ongoing works in progress in the Maker's hands.

Forgiving my ex-husband enabled me to raise my children in a place of peace and not bitterness. When they were angry with him, my anger was not fueled. (Most times anyway). When they brought their frustrations to me, I was able to see the real issue a little more clearly without my own frustrations clouding my judgment. I wanted them to be raised in a place of empathy and compassion. Not a place where their momma was belittling their daddy. I needed to be consistent and steadfast. Always ready and willing to talk to them about their feelings and respond with true honesty. My actions have fostered a close bond with my children. It hasn't always been easy. And, I still tend to drill issues into the ground. They will forgive me for that. I wanted to honor my children with honesty and love. It was an equation that paid off.

Chapter 12
Seeing the Light

I BUSTED THROUGH college in three years including student teaching! Thank goodness I had a sister that was a teacher, too. She was such a Godsend in times of trouble. I took as many hours as humanly possible every semester and went through the summers, too. I missed out on vacations and going out with friends. But, I had a huge goal in mind. The kids loved the fact that their mom was in school. I took Paisley with me every once in a while. Those days are some of our favorite memories. I left before the kids woke up in the morning, and I was home a little after they returned from school. Then, it was momma time, the best time. Homework, playtime, reading, and sometimes just loafing around, these were our days. Finally, after what seemed like forever, I graduated…with honors too! It was an amazing feat coming from a strong C-average high school student that failed geometry not once, but twice! The same week I graduated, I got my first teaching job. The sense of pride I felt, after so many years unable to support my kids, was tremendous. I did it! We all did it!

During that time, I learned how to take fish off the line and build massive amounts of Legos. I learned to laugh again and live again. I learned that love is the strongest emotion that has ever been created, and I love my little family with every ounce of my being. I learned real gratitude for my parents for allowing me to live with them, and for loving me when I'm sure I was very hard to love. I learned what it's like to walk in confidence with Christ.

So many people skirt through life. They don't really know how bad it can be. But, then again, they don't know how good it can be, either. They don't know the feeling of being supported by family and friends through prayer and laughter. Or what it's like to be in such agony that you know your next step may be a stumble, so you fall into the Father's arms. They don't understand how to spot the miracles that the Lord sends during those times because they don't have eyes to see.

This is my story. It is unique only to me. So many others have stories to tell. You have your own demons, which you wrestle with night after night. You may have felt the sting and isolation of lies and abandonment. You may walk crippled with bitterness and despair. This world is full of so much hate, sin, anger, and loneliness. But, this world is not the end. It is the beginning of forever. Walking through fire helps put an eternal perspective in your sights. It sparks hope and faith. I can now say that I have been tested to the very brink of my existence, and with Jesus I have landed on my feet. It fills me with such confidence. We are daughters of a gracious and Heavenly King. He has not created us so that we will give up. We were not made to wallow in our sorrows. He has better plans for us. So, sister, get on your feet and continue moving forward. There are adventures to be had. It's time to bounce back.

Part Two

Bounce Back Life Lessons

Life Lessons

SO MUCH HAS happened since the beginning of my story. As life does, it continually moves on, and so did I. I chose to live the life that the sweet Lord has given me, and not wallow in the pit of lost regrets of what could've, should've, would've been.

I have scars from past hurts, and that's okay. They are sometimes tender and need attention, but all in all they have healed. I used to think they were ugly, but not anymore. I see them as badges of honor because I survived the attack. I didn't go under.

I'm not the only one that notices I have been to hell and back. When I see others who have walked the same path as me, we instantly know each other. We can tell it from the battle wounds and in the depth in our eyes that when you've been to the breaking point and survive, it leaves it's mark. And from those scars, I see what I am made of. I see the pieces of me that are stitched back together again in the way that only God can.

I can't believe it myself sometimes, but I actually got remarried. My husband, Michael, actually asked to be part of this ride and I overwhelmingly accepted. Our lives have truly been an adventure since the first day we met. Being able to come alongside him with my kids in tow was one of the most gracious gifts that my Father in Heaven has given to me.

We added our son, Louie, to the mix a couple of years after we were married. Now we are a family of 5 with a dog and fish, too. Paisley and Edison are now both teenagers, and being their mom is one of my greatest honors. Although I still worry about them as every mother does; my mind doesn't go round and round with fear that the decisions of their father will ruin their lives. If anything, it has made them empathetic, compassionate and loving in ways beyond their years.

I loved college so much that I went back again and got my master's degree. Sometimes I can't even recognize my own self. Everything turned out so different than I thought when I was a little girl. So much better, that is.

This is the exact life that I thought was a figment so many years ago. Although I would find myself dreaming about getting married and having this family, I also knew that it wasn't guaranteed. Nothing ever is. But, to be able to witness how far I've come, really, how far we have come is nothing short of amazing. We are all walking miracles.

~~~~~

I began writing blogs a couple of years ago to share my story with others. At first, I thought they would only be about the divorce, but they have turned into so much more. They encompass childhood memories, parenting, marriage, faith and sometimes just thoughts to ponder. They are pieces of me on a page...my bounce back lessons that I have learned and continue to learn on this life journey. I hope it brings you encouragement and hope in a world that is dry to feeling.

I could not be who I am without my past, but I can't become who I want to be without embracing it. It's me, and I wouldn't have it any other way.

~~~~

In all this you greatly rejoice, though now for a little while you may have had to suffer grief in all kinds of trials. These have come so that the proven genuineness of your faith—of greater worth than gold, which perishes even though refined by fire—may result in praise, glory and honor when Jesus Christ is revealed. Though you have not seen him, you love him; and even though you do not see him now, you believe in him and are filled with an inexpressible and glorious joy, for you are receiving the end result of your faith, the salvation of your souls.

—1 Peter 1:6-9

Lesson 1
The Power of Trust

BEING BETRAYED BY someone we love and trust is crushing. It makes us feel like we never want to trust anyone again. Why would we? It hurts too much. But, we know if we are to truly bounce back, we've got to learn to trust and that can be scary. It starts with trusting God. He is always faithful. Slowly but surely, you will discover that even if others aren't perfect, we are made to connect through trust. This might be the hardest bounce back principle for you, but trust me, it's so worth it.

Broken Is Beautiful

"The best way to find out if you can trust somebody is to trust them." —Ernest Hemingway

~~~~

I WAS TALKING on the phone with one of my best friends from high school while the kids played on the floor. We were just about to hang up when she suddenly interjected that she thought she found a guy she wanted me to meet. *Ummmm ... does she remember that months ago I went through a terrible, heart wrenching, devastating divorce? Does she understand I have NO intention of dating anyone ... maybe ever again!* I told her I thought she was crazy and there was no way I would be interested. She persisted, and continued telling me how awesome he was. *Why don't you date him if he's so great?* She finally accepted that I was not interested, but told me his name anyway ... Michael Carpino. His name was so *Italian!* I repeated his name out loud. Paisley looked up at me with a funny smile on her face and said, "Mom, he's my gym teacher!"

Yes, yes it was true. The same guy that my friend was telling me about was also my daughter's gym teacher. *What are the chances? Ewwww!* And it certainly didn't change the fact that I wasn't interested at all. For me, dating was like to going to the dentist. It was a game I wanted no part of, and I rarely even thought about it. I was ultra-focused on completing school and making sure my kids didn't implode from past events.

Additionally, I was allowing my heart to heal. I felt like I had been hit by a bus, run over several times, and then hung up by my toes. It takes time to get past such soul penetrating pain. There is no time limit … it happens when it happens, and you can't force it.

My life had been broken into two parts: pre-divorced Shannon, who was trusting and naïve, and post-divorce Shannon, who looked at everyone with distrusting eyes. If I was ever to move *past* the terrible memories, I knew I would have to walk *through* them. I would have to feel the ugly, hurtful, crushing parts. I couldn't numb them by going out with men or keeping busy. I had to feel the weight of the loss. Sometimes I felt life would crush me … but somehow it didn't. People are able to handle way more than they think they can.

I had to learn some things, too. I had to learn to listen to my inner voice, and when I saw little red flags in people, I started to listen to my gut instead of assuming the best of people, kind of sad, huh. I started to see things as they were: good *and* bad. I started to trust my own judgment and, really, *myself.* I had lost my self-confidence with the divorce, partially because of what my ex-husband did, but also because I *chose* to marry him. *Is there something in me that attracts people like this? Why didn't I ask him more questions? How did I let it get this far?* These questions gnawed at me. Some of the questions had answers and some of them didn't. But I *did* notice that if I dwelled on them too long, they kept me in the past. Those self-interrogations didn't allow me to learn, which would then allow me to move forward.

I took what I learned and started putting it to good use. I learned to recognize people for who they were instead of who I *wanted* them to be. The more I did it, the easier it got. Something that was good for me to notice was that my ex-husband did not have any long-term friendships, which to me meant more than five years. He didn't have people that knew him inside and out…warts and all. He had no one that challenged him. When people *really* got to know him, they saw the cracks. I never thought about it until after my divorce, but then it became glaringly obvious. I had the support of my friends, and he did not. But, it wasn't because of *what* he did; it was because of *who* he was.

It took me years to go through the process of trusting again. I *had* to trust God in a way that I never had before. I handed Him all of my broken pieces, and allowed Him to put them back together again based on *His* timing … *His* way.

Throughout the years, since my friend brought up the name Michael Carpino, they always teased me about him being out there in the world. We laughed because I never dated anyone, and then someone would say, *"Well, there's always Michael Carpino, the gym teacher!"* I often picked up the kids from school. I would see him in the car line. It was hilarious.

Eventually, more than three years after my friend told me about Michael Carpino, the gym teacher, she finally convinced me to meet him. *What am I doing? This is my kid's gym teacher!* On the other hand, I thought: *Well, he's a teacher, which means he has passed a federal background check. That's a plus.* Don't judge me! It's what anyone would think in my situation.

I didn't want to be alone with Michael; I didn't know him. My friend arranged for us to meet at a party. I picked up my friend from her house. She immediately was disappointed in my outfit. I had no idea why. I wanted to portray a very conservative woman, so I had on a wool turtleneck that looked like I was going hiking in the Himalayas. She convinced me to change and I dressed in a black long sleeve shirt with some dangly earrings. I had to admit; at least I didn't look 80 years old.

We drove to the restaurant where the party was being held, and I saw him walking into the restaurant. My friend pointed him out and we both screamed. *Why? Who knows why girls scream when they see boys ... even girls in their late 20s!*

I could not believe I was going to a party to meet a man. We walked in and my friend introduced us, and it was so ...

easy. I doubt that's the word most people would expect to hear about a first date. And 'easy' was exactly what I needed. We laughed and told stories. It was the best night. It was the beginning.

God has a way of bringing people into our lives exactly when He's ready. As time progressed, I learned more about Michael. He showed a heart for people and was a man of God. He was honest. It was so refreshing. If he said he was going to do something, he did. There were no tricks or manipulations. No riddles. It just flowed. He earned my trust and always handled it with care. I trusted Michael because I trusted in the Lord to heal my heart. Michael loved me for just being me. I never felt judged by my past, but loved because I had come through it.

Remember how I felt about him being the gym teacher? God, in his perfect design, knew if I could be comfortable around any man, he would have to pass the kid test. My kids had known him longer than I had. Paisley was in second grade when we met.

We married about a year after we met. It was as if I had come full circle. Looking back, I truly believe that God allowed my friend to bring up Michael's name during that phone conversation so many years ago. It was almost as if God was saying: *Look what I have for you. Great things are coming, but not until you are ready.*

If you have been hurt, you are not damaged beyond repair. Don't feel as if you are incapable of moving forward and regaining your ability to trust people. God has mighty work to do in you before you can take those steps. Surround yourself with people that have proven themselves trustworthy. While you are working through things, bounce ideas off them. They can help you. Learn from your past mistakes. If a choice turned out poorly, don't do it again. The more good choices you make, the more you will trust your instincts. However, never forget; the best thing to do is pray! Pray to Jesus for guidance in everything. He will help you discern the best choices. You are that special to Him; He won't leave you scattered in pieces. He will bring you back together again. You are not broken. You're beautiful.

~~~~

You will keep in perfect peace those whose minds are steadfast, because they trust in you.

—Isaiah 26:3

Lesser Life

"Listen to the mustn'ts, child. Listen to the don'ts. Listen to the shouldn'ts, the impossibles, the won'ts. Listen to the never haves, then listen close to me ... Anything can happen, child. Anything can be." —*Shel Silverstein*

~~~~

HAVE YOU EVER felt like the world keeps trying to put us in little categories according to our life circumstances? It throws statistics at us, which tell us what our lives should look like according to a poll or a study. How many times do we hear on the nightly news "According to the blah-blah poll, X percent of Americans ...?" It's like they try to plug us into little equations so they can see the probability of the outcome.

Single mom + two kids = disaster

Or

Teenager + life = out of control

Neither statement can possibly be true all of the time. Sometimes single moms *do* have disasters on their hands, and sometimes teenagers *are* out of control, but not all the time. And, this is certainly not the way it *has* to be.

When I was newly divorced, my parents gave me an encouragement book made just for me … single mom. One night, after the children were in bed, I thought I would take a hot bath and relax. I noticed the book sitting, and I thought 'What the heck. I could use some encouragement.' I put my hair up and got cozy in the bath. I reached for my book, took a deep breath, and began to read. The first story was about a single mother that had to work two jobs to put food on the table. Because she was gone so much, her son rebelled and began stealing. He was eventually arrested and was sent to jail. His mom now visits him there, but he has forgiven her for having to work so much.

Ummmmm … so, not feeling very encouraged here. Feeling a little *stressed* at the moment. But, hey, they can't all be like that. I read the next one.

The next story described the plight of a single mom whose husband abandoned her and her daughter. Her daughter became so overwrought with grief she became a drug addict. However, after a 10-year addiction, the mother and daughter came through to the other side and had a better relationship for it.

Whoa. Now, please don't get me wrong. These stories all had redemptive qualities, and many people could connect with them. But, it was not exactly what I was looking for in a book of encouragement for single mothers. I was looking for fluffy, happy stories. But, what I got was what the world tells us. The world tells us that children of divorce are doomed to a life of "lesser." Less happiness, less education, less overall satisfaction in life. So, if they are already doomed then why try, right?

Wrong! I was not about to accept that fate for my children. There was something that the world was not betting on. Something forgotten in its equation: *Jesus.*

It was then and there, in that cold bathtub, I decided my children didn't belong to the world. I had always known that, but I actually *declared* it that night. I declared that they belonged to Jesus Christ, King of Kings, and with His help they would not become statistics.

We are all new creations with Jesus. Your life circumstances do not matter. You could be the drug addict, the abused, the abuser, the control freak, the rage addict, the enabler, the prostitute, or the liar … it doesn't matter. You plug all those things into the world's equation and you get despair. You get an empty life full of regret. You get hopelessness. But, if you include *Jesus*, you get a completely different outcome. You get love and a peace, which can't be described. You get acceptance. You get a faith that carries you through your journey. And what you *were* doesn't define you anymore because you are entirely, solely *new* in Jesus.

The world offers us the "lessers" and tells us it is all we are worth. It suggests that our circumstances define us, telling us this is as good as it gets. But, don't buy it. It's a lie. Jesus loved us so much that He died for us … no matter what our story. He *chose* to die for us. And He longs to be able to show you how amazing your life will be.

~~~~

Therefore, if anyone is in Christ, the new creation has come: The old has gone, the new is here!

—2 Corinthians 5:17

Second Chances

"Miracles were just second chances if you really thought about it--second chances when all hope was lost." —Kaya McLaren, How I Came to Sparkle Again

~~~~

OH MY GOSH! I went on a date, and I had a really, *really* good time! Later, I was lying in my bed thinking I should be totally excited. It has been a VERY long time since I had a date. I had not had a date since I got divorced. A lot of people had encouraged me to date thinking it would help me get over my situation. And, yes, I did get asked out every now and then. But, no one seemed interesting enough to compete with the precious little time I could spend with my children. Plus, I needed that God-given time to heal from the divorce.

But, now it felt a little different. This guy, Michael, was different. And, he had already asked me out *AGAIN! What is this going to be like? What if he is a freak like a stalker or a weirdo? What if he lies to me like my ex-husband? What if I'm a mess, and I've forgotten how to trust someone?* The night that held such promise was causing me to become a ball of nerves.

I stared at the ceiling as my mind raced. I prayed to Jesus. I really wanted His blessing. It had taken me years ... I'm not exaggerating ... *YEARS* to work through the issues of my divorce. *I forgave my ex-husband a long time ago, but what if the effects of his actions bleed into my new relationships?* I tried to think of every possible scenario, and I tried to think how I would handle it. It was not just me; I had my kids to think of. And I didn't think I could lead them down a path that could cause their little hearts to be broken ... *again.* This time everything would be on my shoulders. *Is any of this even worth it?* I spilled my guts to Jesus. I was a big ole mess, and I was speaking a mile a minute. Suddenly, almost as if He'd had enough, He decides to interrupt me. I had an overwhelming feeling like He was telling me, *"Shannon, its okay."* And, that was all I needed to hear.

I took it step by step ... day by day. I had to be extremely careful to not put my ex-husband's sins on Michael. If an issue came up that would cause me to feel unsettled, I brought it to his attention and we would talk about it. For example, the cell phone was a major problem with my ex-husband. He would talk with people he shouldn't have been talking to, hide it from me, and then tell me I was crazy for not trusting him. When I communicated this to Michael, he was a complete open book. He wasn't mad or frustrated. He was very understanding. He said he didn't want to have any secrets between us. What is mine is yours, and you can see it whenever you like. So, because of that, I never felt the need to be looking over his shoulder because his actions were so transparent. It was an entirely new experience. It was like it was supposed to be. It's amazing what the healing power of forgiveness and the Lord can do for a person. Baggage can be lifted and washed away. Feelings I thought I would have I really didn't. The Lord was right, *it was okay*. Needless to say, one date led to another, and then to another. Yes, this wonderful honest man full of integrity decided to ask that all of my chaos become his, and I was more than happy to share it.

Michael had never been married before, and he didn't have children. Boy oh boy! Was he in for it! After we married, for some reason he often spoke about how tired he was … funny! Welcome to my world! However, we actually blended pretty well. There were a few bumps here and there, but nothing crazy huge … another answer to prayer.

One night, Michael, had back-to-back softball games. He was in a church league, and sometimes we would watch. However, that night was a school night, and the second game was going to go pretty late, so I decided not to watch in order to get the kids to bed on time. After I got the children settled and I nestled in myself, I heard Eddie's little feet plopping down the stairs. He had a look of real concern on his face. Worry is a terrible look for a six-year-old. He sat next to me on the couch and placed his little hand on my leg. Then he said something that totally boggled my mind. He said, "Mom, do you *really* think that Dad is playing a softball game at night? Most softball games are during the day. It just doesn't make sense, does it?" Oh, my heart just broke for him. I had known *I* would have trust issues because of what we had gone through, but it had never crossed my mind that my children would have trust issues, too! What was I thinking? Goodness!

I called a baby sitter over to the house for Paisley, and took his chubby little hand, put him in the car, and drove to the softball field so he could see his new daddy doing exactly what he said he would be doing. I'll never forget Eddie's face; it showed such relief. He was not going to be fooled again. He was told the truth. That boy has never doubted his dad again. He never had reason to.

The effects of deceit can run so deep, especially when we have been lied to by the ones we trusted the most. It's a pain that penetrates our souls. And, of course, we don't want it to happen again. We don't want to be fooled into feeling like idiots again, so we put up a shield to keep people far enough away so it won't hurt so badly. But, that's no way to live. It prevents us from being close with anyone. We are meant to learn from our past, not to be defined by it. It's okay to take a second chance at things. Trust your gut. If you think someone is not being forthcoming, confront it. The Lord gives us discernment for a reason. Don't be afraid to forgive.

~~~~

Lord my God, I called to you for help, and you healed me. You, Lord, brought me up from the realm of the dead; you spared me from going down to the pit. Sing the praises of the Lord, you his faithful people; praise his holy name.

—Psalms 30:2-4

Making Memories

"October had tremendous possibility. The summer's oppressive heat was a distant memory, and the golden leaves promised a world full of beautiful adventures. They made me believe in miracles." —*Sarah Guillory,* Reclaimed

~~~

HEAR THOSE LEAVES crunching under your feet? Smell the burning logs in the fire pits at night? See the burst of color in the trees before they have to slumber for the winter? Yes, October ... the month that always felt the most familiar to me. I never knew why, but whenever it came, it was like the return of an old friend.

October called me to spend as much time outside as was humanly possible. I wore sweaters in the morning, and then was hot by mid afternoon. I soaked it up as much as I could because I knew winter was lurking, and I didn't leave the house when it was cold. I know, I sound like I'm 95 years old. But, my children could tell you, mom didn't play outside when it was less than 50 degrees.

But one fall weekend we woke to find the most perfect day for some family hiking. I'd never want to paint a false

Norman Rockwell picture. I wasn't in the habit of hiking. But, it was Fall Break, and I wanted to take advantage of having a school holiday.

~~~~

I decided to take my kids to a local state park for the hike. Michael had recently undergone sinus surgery, so he had the perfect excuse to stay behind. I thought the four of us could create a great memory. Perfect October day, nowhere to go, and I have my three kids ... TOGETHER! Mommas with teens, y'all know this is a very big deal!

We parked the car and began our hike. There was a huge shiny map at the base of the parking lot; we all stopped to take a look. I've have always been terribly directionally challenged. I can get lost anywhere. Places where people are not *supposed* to get lost, *I* get lost. So, when I looked at the map, all I could see were little squiggly lines that had dots and slashes. I did see a yellow star that marked "YOU ARE HERE," but it truly meant nothing to me. And, sad to say, I had passed on that genetic disconnect to my daughter, Paisley.

We started to walk. It was like a movie. There was a beautiful scenic lake with a trail alongside. Behind the lake were rolling hills with red, yellow, and orange hues covering the trees. My daughter spotted a little deer nibbling around the fallen leaves. We whispered and took pictures. Look over there! Wild turkeys! My children were laughing together and holding hands! It was working! We were making memories that would last forever! Until ...

The youngest, Louie, said he was thirsty. I hadn't thought we'd be hiking long, so I hadn't brought any food or drink. He asked how long we'd been gone, and my daughter said one hour. An hour! We had to walk back an hour? Which way did we come from? Does this look familiar to anyone? Louie's imagination went into overdrive; he was sure we would die there, out in the wilderness. Other hikers would find our skeletons on the trail. Paisley and I started to freak out. We were talking 100 words per second, spinning in circles and trying to figure out where we had come from or where to go. Then, Eddie, said, "Guys, I know where to go. I looked at the map. All the trails are in a circle. Let's just continue going the same way." This was a real first for me. Normally, *I* knew what to do. I was the mom after all. *I* usually had the answers. But, this time, I was out of my element. This time *my son* had the answers. He took action, and he had such confidence about him. So we followed him.

There were times that day when we thought he had taken us in the wrong direction, but in the end he was right. He got us exactly where we needed to go. And, as he turned around to flash his dimpled smile, which clearly said he had "saved" us ... 'it' happened. On that October day, the shadow of my boy still stood there, but I also saw the glimmer of the man who was to come. I was so grateful that I was there to witness it. Don't get me wrong ... he still had a loooonnnggg way to go. But, I was seeing him with different eyes. It was truly amazing.

~~~~

I had to be completely out of my realm to trust my son to lead us out of the woods. I knew enough to know that my own abilities couldn't do it, so I had to lean on his knowledge. Isn't that the same with our relationship with the Lord? It usually takes an overwhelming situation, one where we feel totally out of control, before we come to Him for guidance. Often, it is like we are treading water, and we only ask for help from the Lord when we get tired. When, all along, He could get us out of the ocean! He wants to be involved in all aspects of our lives: the goofy, the exciting, the terrifying and the mundane, too! So, why are we waiting?

~~~~

Trust in the Lord with all your heart and lean not on your own understanding; in all your ways submit to Him, and He will make your paths straight.

—Proverbs 3:5-6

Bad Day

"This day had officially punched every hole in her crazy ticket." —Kimberly Kincaid, Drawing the Line

~~~~

I THOUGHT: *This cannot be happening. Not after the week I've had. A couple days ago my car starting making some weird car noise...again. This is the second time this week this has happened! We have already put a lot of money into this car, and it's got something else wrong with it now!*

I pulled into the garage when I got home and immediately went to Michael's office to tell him I thought something was wrong with the car. It was making a *Grrrr ... grrrr ... bang ... bang ... psffffff ...* noise. I had to go through the whole process of answering the husband questions: "What did you do? Did you run over something? I bet you hit the curb again." The answer was no to all of the questions. We called the car shop and made an appointment to bring the car in. *I don't know about your experiences, but when it comes to cars and our family, if we take the car in, it's never a quick fix.* I have never heard "Oh, it's just a cap that fell off." Or "That hose just got a little loose. I fixed it at no charge." We normally hear "Well, this is pretty rare.

We don't know exactly what it is, but its gonna be expensive."

Not only did my car break down this week, my husband's did too. How is this even possible?? No joke, I knew way too much about the garage's receptionist. Since I had been to that shop so often, she and I figured we might as well divulge our personal information.

In addition to our cars, our home air conditioner went out, too. It was not even close to funny; *we live in the south! I don't sparkle, I sweat! My hair is frizzy and unmanageable. Taking away our air conditioning in July is taking away any possibility of a good mood, too.*

But, that wasn't it. That wasn't the final electronic blow. Our technical devices had one more trick up their sleeves ... the dishwasher. I had loaded the dishwasher full of dirty dishes. It was ready to go, and I was so happy to let it do its job. However, when I closed the dishwasher, it started beeping repeatedly—the kind of beeping that means 'stop immediately.' I looked at that machine over and over again. *Maybe it's too full? Maybe I blocked the drain?* I fiddled with it a bit more, and yet that terrible beeping persisted. I looked online to investigate. Of course, exactly what I had predicted; it needed service AND I knew the warranty had expired six months earlier. *Perfect ... PERFECT!!!!! Our cars are broken, we are hot, and now we don't have a dishwasher during the summer time and everyone is home.*

My feelings of frustration were not only about broken things breaking. Things break sometimes. We live in a country where we have luxuries. They are not necessities. The human race has lived a very long time without cars, air conditioning, and dishwashers. It's not about being a Prima donna; I can live in a hot house and do dishes by hand.

The problem was much more than that. I openly and willingly admitted (to myself): *MONEY ANXIETY.*

I am a total recovering money worrier. I admit it. There should be a 12 step-program for people like me...maybe there already is. I really struggle. So, when I see a lot of money going out the door to fix stuff, I relapse.

~~~~

 I wasn't always a money worrier. I used to live carefree in the beautiful bliss of ignorance. But things changed when I became a single mother. I lost most of my belongings. I could not afford to keep our home, gas for the car, and most other items that were not absolutely necessary. Fun things were not part of the new budget. I remember feeling so defeated at the beginning of the new school year when fees were being collected. There were times we couldn't pay. We didn't have the money. Or, when the kiddos wanted fun trinket things, which all the other kids had, but we could not afford. Our lack of funds was a constant reminder that I was unable to full provide for my family. The children didn't mind it as much as I did, but it all stuck with me. I don't ever want to be in that situation again.

Years later I realized I had tricked myself into thinking money offered me security. I had made it an idol. However, if you looked at me from the outside you wouldn't think that. I didn't act like a money hungry mongrel. I didn't shop a lot, or buy the newest things. I didn't withhold money from charities or church. But, it was in my heart. I had always been afraid in situations dealing with money. I'm afraid if I spend too much, I won't have enough. Enough for what I don't know. I could probably never have enough.

Eventually I learned that money could never offer me security. Only God could do that. I know this, but it's something that I continually work through. Money doesn't love me, it doesn't care about my well-being; it has no feeling whatsoever. But, I still willingly give my feelings to it. I drive myself crazy. I know this ... and I've come a long way, too! My poor husband!

I have to remind myself that Jesus can only give me the security I crave. He has constantly taken care of my family and me. My children and I have always had shelter, been fed, and been warm when it's cold or vice versa. What are you putting your security in? Is it money like I have done in the past? Is it your spouse or yourself? If it's not Jesus, you will be let down. You will be exposed to the emotional rollercoaster, which comes with putting your trust in earthly things. We are all works in progress. Let's keep our sights on the One who promised us that we will always be taken care of.

~~~~

*There is no one like the God of Jeshurun, who rides across
the heavens to help you and on the clouds in his majesty.*
—Deuteronomy 33:26

Lesson 2
The Power of Gratitude

GRATITUDE IS ONE of the strongest emotions in the world. But, sometimes it's hard to feel grateful when your world has been rocked and you are looking up from the floor. But if you want to bounce back, this attitude will jump-start your upward climb. The whole world starts looking better when you feel grateful.

Holiday Snapshots

"For each new morning with its light, for rest and shelter of the night, for health and food, for love and friends, for everything Thy goodness sends." —Ralph Waldo Emerson

~~~~

AHHHH! SNUGGLED ON the couch to watch one of the best Christmas movies EVER ... *It's A Wonderful Life*. Gosh, this movie brings back some comfy feelings of my childhood. My parents still watch it every New Year's Eve. It's a movie that lacks color ... yes, its black and white. I fuss at the kids saying, "Some of the best movies are black and white, y'all!" The end always gets me ... *spoiler alert* (and really, if you haven't seen it by now, then I can't help you!): When George sees a glimpse of what life would be without him, he begins to understand how much of an impact one person can make in the lives of others. And that truly, he is so loved and appreciated. He learns that life would not have been better without him; and he sees that many people are completely grateful for him. No kidding ... tears every time.

I know, I know, it's Christmas time, and I should be writing about the hustle and bustle or sweet baby Jesus's birth, but this week, I'm still stuck on the feeling of gratefulness. And, honestly, isn't that a Christmas quality, too?

Yes, when I think of gratefulness, my thinking seems to move toward the generic things like health and family. But, the more I started thinking about gratefulness, the more I started seeing it in different ways. I started thinking about those who don't have their health and don't have family. The good Lord doesn't guarantee life with those gifts. What would I do without those things? Would I be less grateful? It made me really think about what I was truly ... I mean *TRULY* thankful for.

And, when I dare imagined myself without my health and family, I start thinking about what parts of life, what parts of the big picture, filled my heart. Of course, my first thought was my eternal salvation through Jesus. That is a gift that I cannot buy, but just receive with open hands. And, knowing that my Heavenly Father has a place for me when my days are over has me swimming in gratitude. *But, what about life in the here and now? The everyday things?*

I think about the gifts that the Lord gives us all ... all humankind. I think about scenes that offer me comfort. One of the first images I had was of a summer day when a storm was slowly coming in. I love going outside and watching the purple clouds move with every gust of wind. The smell of approaching rain fills my nose, and the warm air moves around me. I stand and just ... *feel*. I hear the chimes hanging from the tree, and the rise and fall of the leaves blowing. It is one of the very REAL things I am grateful for. I also find myself thankful for the emotion of laughter, the kind of laughter that hurts your belly, and for those who have delivered babies, makes us wet our pants! I love how laughter just makes things better. It has the power to totally change a person's attitude, or bring people together when they have experiences they laugh over. You can bring up those memories and laugh again and again! It's the gift that keeps on giving! Or walking barefoot with the grass beneath my feet, hugging an old friend, listening to a beautiful piece of music, or seeing individual snowflakes. I feel like I should be Julie Andrews singing "Favorite Things" from the *Sound of Music*! But, really, these are things that the Lord gives us all. These little 'snapshots of the eternal' give us a glimpse of what is to come in Heaven. I think of these things ... and because I am blessed to have children and a family, I want to share these things with them. Life is so good.

I hope and pray that during this Christmas time, we don't overlook the simple things. We get so caught up in the season, we often miss the fact that everyday should be Christmas—when we see what the Lord has done.

~~~~

Let the peace of Christ rule in your hearts, since as members of one body you were called to peace, and be thankful.

—Colossians 3:15

Sick Kid Denial

Sick kids almost never go to their father's side of the bed to announce they're going to barf. —Julie Ann Barnhill

~~~~

"I HAVE A sore throat, Mom," Louie says. I hear him, but I can't see him because my eyes are shut. Why, you may ask. Well, my eyes are shut because I'm in bed still asleep. It literally takes effort, *real* effort, to open them. He is standing five millimeters from my face. I feel his hot, germy breath on my nose. When my eyes focus, I also notice that my little guy has that sick look. That pasty green look that makes you think they are going to throw up any second. My first thought is I better get out of the way because he may puke on me; my other thought is to check his throat. Yep, I bet its strep. With him being my third child, I can smell strep a mile away. *Great!*

On top of that, we have had a billion snow days this year. Having a snow day here and there is really fun. We pull out the snow boots, get some good movies, snuggle up with hot chocolate with extra marshmallows and enjoy! But, when you have more snow days than you know what to do with, home can become an ice prison! All the kids at home, at the same time, day after day, hour after hour, minute after minute, *second ... after ... second ...*

~~~~

We were just getting our groove back. School was in for a full two days! Yay consistency! But, it suddenly came to screeching halt. So, to the doctor we go and yep, strep it is ... *surprise!* Then, comes the shot fight. It's familiar to ALL families. It's a kid's immediate automatic response to being at the doctor's office. It always ends with a tear-streaked face, a mad momma, and a nurse that just wants to get the heck out of there. Poor things ... the nurses ... not the kid!

The next morning I was in complete denial about Louie having to stay home. I woke him up with full intention of sending him to school, until his dad reminded me of the whole "germ" issue. *Whaaaat? Contagious? 24 hours? I mean, is that a real thing?* He had no fever! He was bouncing off the walls wanted me to chase him ... he put silly putty on my computer screen ... need I go on? So, no, I didn't send him. *You're welcome all of the kids in Louie's class.* And, honestly, I was super frustrated that I had only one more day until spring break to get my things done. But there was a child at home. As moms, *our* time is so precious. We guard it, we protect it!

But, the more I thought about it, the more I realized how selfish I was being. I thought about how blessed I was that I had the *ability* to stay home with a sick child. I haven't always been able to do that with my children. It was my hand that was brushing his blonde hair aside, and my arms were cuddling him. There are a lot of mommas that would love to care for their sick children, but circumstances don't allow it. I paused to reflect on how grateful I was to be able to be part of *all* the days, the healthy ones and the unhealthy ones...the good ones and the bad. And, it made me happy I was there to do it.

~~~~

Children are a heritage from the Lord, offspring a reward from him.

—Psalm 127:3

A Thanksgiving Day Lesson

But Thanksgiving is more than eating, Chuck. You heard what Linus was saying out there. Those early Pilgrims were thankful for what had happened to them, and we should be thankful, too. We should just be thankful for being together. I think that's what they mean by 'Thanksgiving,' Charlie Brown. —Marcie, A Charlie Brown Thanksgiving

~~~~

"WHERE'S THE DOG??" I remember my mom asking my dad as we were packing for a holiday trip with my family in Atlanta when I was about thirteen years old. That's when I heard it. The noise of paw claws on wood. I followed the noise into the kitchen where I saw the dog on its tiptoes, stretching as far as his nose would go, trying to get his mouth around the tasty treasure of the heavenly ham leftovers from last night's dinner. He hadn't quite gotten it yet; but when he heard us, it gave him the energy to jump a bit further, and he was successful. He had a massively huge ham in his mouth. I was surprised that his two back feet hadn't lifted off the ground as he started to run with it through the house. There we were; all of us chasing that dog through the house as his legs moved way faster than our feet could possibly go. They moved so fast it was a blur to watch! We all laughed so hard, we had to stop chasing him. It was mayhem ... beautiful, glorious chaos, which always surrounds that time of year.

At the start of each new holiday season, many of us start to feel the fingers of stress tighten around our throats and chest, and it becomes hard to breathe. *Why does this happen?* I understand *why,* but I guess the real question I'm asking is: *Why do we allow it to happen?* Is it the pressure we put on ourselves, or is it the pressure we allow others to put on us? Is it seeing people we haven't seen in a while that sparks healed wounds to ooze and old emotional injuries to throb? Maybe it's all of the above.

So many times, as women, we think we should have an epic Hollywood version of what a holiday should be like. Everybody comes over to a clean house where the children, who have been classically trained in piano, are giving a recital while the dinner is being cooked. Miraculously, the desserts, side dishes, AND the turkey all finished cooking at the exact same time, and are ALL bubbly golden brown. Then, as all family members sit down together at a Martha Stewart decorated table, *with nameplates*, we hold hands and go around the table and express our deepest gratitude for all our blessings. Then, as a family, we all enjoy a gratifying feast together ... *And then we wake up from our dream*! We build up massive expectations, which in no possible way could ever be met. When those massive expectations are not met, everything comes crashing down on us like a 100,000-pound drumstick!

Many American holidays look like this: Family members come to the door, hopefully sober, and the kids are fighting over what TV show to watch. As things boil over on the stove and the casserole burns, someone throws up on the kitchen floor and has to be quarantined. When we finally sit down, we find a hodgepodge table of mix and match dishes and silverware, and then let out a scream that we forgot the rolls in the oven, which then sets off the fire alarm. That's life!

But life is full of the unexpected. It's the unexpected that makes for the best stories. If life were perfect, wouldn't it be boring? We try to bring together those who have made an impact in our lives. Sometimes the impact is good, sometimes not, but either way our lives are shaped by our family experiences. Holiday get-togethers are a perfect opportunity to show Jesus to your family. It is a time to show patience, love, and hospitality. If we expect people to behave the same way they have behaved for the past 20 years, then wouldn't we have a better holiday season? We can't control how others behave, but we can control how we react to them.

I'm not guaranteed how many holidays I'll have with my children. In fact, until they are 18 years-old they HAVE to spend the holidays with me. They can't run somewhere else. But after that, who knows? Single parents may have even less holiday time with their children. Don't you want your children to remember these times with laughter and fondness? Don't you want them to say, "Remember when…?" Children watch your reactions. The holidays are a great time to soak up the family, hold them close. Days turn into months, and months turn into years, and before you know it, what we knew is gone. Live in the moment, and truly be thankful for all we have.

~~~~

Therefore, since we are receiving a kingdom that cannot be shaken, let us be thankful, and so worship God acceptably with reverence and awe.

—*Hebrews 12:28*

A Story of Gratitude

Dear old world," she murmured, "you are very lovely, and I am glad to be alive in you." —L.M. Montgomery, Anne of Green Gables

~~~~

I HEARD A story of a man who lost his daughter from an illness when she was just 16 years old. The little girl he had held the day she was born. Her smile made his heart flutter. She laughed at his silly jokes. She was gone. He would never see her get a driver's license and drive away towards her freedom. He didn't get to see her graduate high school, nor help her choose a college. He would never walk her down the aisle and feel the pride of giving her away. Tragic. Understandably, he was in the throws of depression and grief. Every day was difficult; her absence made no sense. Thankfully, he was a man of God and sought guidance from his pastor. His pastor asked one question, which changed the man's life forever. He asked, "If you would've known that your daughter would only live 16 years, would you have rather not had her and not have the grief, or was she worth the grief that you are feeling now?"

The man knew exactly what the pastor was saying. We are not guaranteed anything in this life, and we don't know how long the people we love are going to be with us. The man looked at his pastor and said, "I'd rather have 16 years with her than *any* without her." And, in that instant, gratefulness filled the man's heart. He had the privilege of knowing and loving his most precious daughter for 16 years, and he wouldn't trade it for the world ... even knowing he would face so much grief at the end of her life.

Gratitude is an amazing emotion. It can be used in so many ways. It can turn a tragedy into something meaningful. It can bring a healthy perspective, and it can truly show the depth of the human heart.

We call the holidays the season of gratitude. And, it's true. This time of year *does* make us reflect on gratitude. We surround ourselves with family and friends we may not often see. We travel, and we participate in yearly traditions. We stay up late talking and catching up. It really is a time to swim in gratitude.

But, why wait until the holiday season? Why do we wait to focus on the Lord's gifts for just this time of year? Gratitude has power when we allow ourselves to be cradled in the Heavenly Father's arms. We should rest easy knowing that He has given us all the provision that we need. He doesn't wait until Thanksgiving, He does it daily. But we neglect to see it as often as we do during the holiday season.

Allow yourself to feel gratitude all year long. It's not meant for only one season.

If you are having a difficult time finding even small things to be grateful for, you may need to start at the beginning. You have breath in your lungs, and you are meant to be here. Life may have been difficult for you. You may have many scars. But, you are *here*. You survived. You see, you have an amazing Savior that chose to die for you because He loved you. That's it. You were worth His sacrifice. He loved you so much, not because of anything you *did*, but because of who you *are*. He died to give you life eternal. That's really the greatest love there is. You now have hope and expectation. You now have purpose and meaning. It doesn't matter about your past or your future. You are free in Christ. It's truly a gift. That's something to be grateful for every day.

~~~~

Rejoice always, pray continually, give thanks in all circumstances; for this is God's will for you in Christ Jesus.

—1 Thessalonians 5:16-18

Great Expectations

"Don't set your expectations too high so your life will be successful." —Edison Carpino

~~~~

THIS QUOTE CAME from my then 14-year-old son, Eddie. We were on the way home from school, and we started talking about senior quotes in the yearbook, the quotes seniors put under their picture so we can see a glimpse into their 18-year-old brains. Some quotes were funny, some quirky, some prophetic ... you get the picture. I asked Eddie what his quote would be, and without even thinking about it, he said, "Don't set your expectations so high, and then your life will be successful."

At first, I rolled my eyes and laughed. Really Eddie? That's the imprint you want to leave in the yearbook? Of course, when Eddie said that, he meant it in the teenager way. He meant the less responsibility he had, the better. He was under the impression he would always feel successful without ever having to do anything. We had a good laugh. Oh Eddie.

But, the more I thought about Eddie's quote, the more I agreed with him. Except ... of course, not in the way Eddie meant it. We so often have crazy high expectations of our-selves, those around us, and, well, life in general. We want everything to be perfect, easy, and to unfold exactly the way we planned. So ... has that *EVER* happened? Has any project ever been *easy*? Has life been *exactly* the way you planned it? Let me answer that question for you ... **NO!**

However, when we don't reach our expectation, we are of-ten disappointed. We pout and sometimes even pitch a grown-up fit. It's not fair! It's not how I thought it would be! Consider instead taking a moment to reflect on your life and how it *did* turn out. I have had some real roller coaster moments, but I am soooo happy it <u>didn't</u> work out the way I had planned. It turned out WAY better! And although I still have expectations, I'm okay if they don't pan out the way I planned. The Lord knows what I need so much more than I do, and I am glad of that!

~~~~

For I know the plans I have for you, declares the Lord, plans for welfare and not for evil, to give you a future and a hope.

—Jeremiah 29:11

Life Lesson 3
The Power to Overcome

WE WILL GET knocked down in life. It's guaranteed. But, you have a choice to bounce back. You may feel tired and powerless, just like I did. But, you are stronger than you think. Start with faith and God—if He's on your side what can anyone do to stop you? It won't take long to discover you are a survivor and a thriver as you bounce back up!

Why Me?

"Don't try to make life a mathematics problem with your-self in the center and everything coming out equal. When you're good, bad things can still happen. And if you're bad, you can still be lucky." —Barbara Kingsolver, The Poisonwood Bible

~~~~

LIFE IS COMPLETELY, utterly, and unassumingly terribly unfair. I know this statement is not a shocker to anyone, but sometimes it just needs to be said. I often want to stomp my foot, cross my arms, and give life the stink eye because it doesn't make sense. Children are orphaned, people are victimized, health is compromised, and opportunities don't present themselves. It's just not right.

But, for some reason, we are continually shocked at this simple fact. When life hands us our portion of unfairness we become totally confused about how this could have happened to us. To *US*? Bad things happen to other people, right? **WRONG!**

When my ex-husband and I were going through our divorce, I was in an absolute state of … well, I was in a lot of different states. I was in a state of shock, denial, depression to name a few. There were so many layers to my divorce. I would discover something and begin to accept it; but then I would peel back *another* layer of deceit and discover something else. Each new discovery caused my heart to feel as if it would stop beating. Blood would rush to my head, and I would relive the pain once again. It seemed like the layers would never end. And, in my case, it happened fast so I didn't have a lot of time to get used to the fact that I was going to be a single mom.

One day, I was sitting in my parent's house (which little did I know it would soon become home to my children and me), and I was having a pity party. And, to be honest, I was enjoying it. I was letting the victim mentality spill all over me. And why shouldn't I? I was having such a terrible time. I *was* a victim. It *wasn't* fair! I looked over at my father, who was sitting in his comfy recliner chair, and I asked, "Why me? Why did this have to happen to *me*?" I was hoping he would fill my bruised and battered ego and defend me. But, my manipulation didn't work. He looked directly at me, shrugged his shoulders, and said, "Why *not* you?"

Whoa...wait what? Did he just totally ignore my plea for pity? Why, yes he did!

I was beyond frustrated. It happens when we get challenged, doesn't it? "What the heck does that mean?" I asked. What he said next may seem harsh, but it was real truth. He told me that simply because I was a believer does not make me exempt from the life's underbelly. Plus, wouldn't I rather something like this happen to me because I had the Lord and my family to lean into? There were people out there alone and going through harsh times. They didn't have faith or hope. They face their obstacles in despair.

I felt as if his words had slapped me in the face. I was speechless. I sat in silence to allow his words to sink in. He was speaking life to me instead of allowing me to swim in the life-is-unfair pool. No longer could I see myself as a victim, or as someone who had been dealt a bad marriage hand. I had to accept my lot and see it as a way for the Lord to change and grow me. And, boy oh boy, did He. After I arrived on the other side of that terrible moment, I could truly say, with 100 percent honesty, that my divorce was one of the most God-centered points of my life. My faith was tested, and I can tell you this: the Lord's promises are true.

The "Why Not Me" philosophy can translate into any aspect of life: marriage, sickness, death, love, infertility, ANYTHING! It allows us to accept our circumstances at face value and meet our challenges head on instead of being distracted with life's unfairness. It gives us a teachable heart and allows us to learn from our situations instead of a bitter heart full of frustration. If you find yourself asking "Why me?" turn it around! Ask "Why not me?" You will soon discover you are quite equipped to handle the situation and bounce back. Plus, Lord is there to carry you through.

~~~~

Blessed is the one who perseveres under trial because, having stood the test, that person will receive the crown of life that the Lord has promised to those who love him.

—James 1:12

Fourth Grade Problems

"I prefer to be true to myself, even at the hazard of incurring the ridicule of others, rather than to be false, and to incur my own abhorrence." —*Frederick Douglass*

~~~~

ONE AFTERNOON WHEN school was over, Paisley came into my classroom with an incredibly sad expression on her little face. One of the perks of being a teacher in the same school your kids attend is if the child has a problem, he or she can go quickly to Mom. Paisley slung her backpack on top of a desk, slumped into a chair, and let out a massive sigh.

I was behind my desk getting my things together so we could leave for the day. Papers needed to be taken home and graded and it required a bit of order; plus I couldn't stand arriving in the morning to a messy desk.

Paisley glanced at me; she hadn't received the reaction she was seeking. Soon she let out another sigh, but she also added the arched back and slouched chair position. It was too dramatic to ignore.

"What's going on, Paisley?" I asked

"Mom, I'm having trouble in class," she said.

"What kind of trouble?"

"Well," she said, "I keep cheating! I know it's wrong, but I just can't help it! The teacher has me sitting too close to the other kids.

Okay, I thought. On one hand, I was really happy she was telling me about the cheating and that she felt bad about it. I've always wanted an open and honest relationship with my kids, and I have encouraged transparency at all costs. But, on the other hand, *she was cheating*! And at the school where I was teaching! My daughter's teacher was my co-worker! *Geez!*

Oh my gosh! I could totally envision her little eyes darting toward her neighbor's desk. I could see her little sweaty hand writing down the answer from someone else's paper. *What could I do?* I decided to act super cool about it. Not too cool so it might make her suspicious, but just cool enough.

I didn't overreact. I acted distracted, and asked only one question. "So, what are you going to do about it?"

She said that she already had an answer. She had thought about it long and hard and had a plan. She was going to tell the teacher to move her during tests so she wouldn't be tempted. Wow! That's a great idea, I thought. My little girl was growing up and learning how to deal with her own problems. Proud moment...although she was a cheater I was happy she felt guilty. *C'mon y'all, we have got to take the successes when they come.*

Nonetheless, the following day she came again to my classroom and yelled, "I did it again! She didn't move me far away enough!"

Are you kidding me? I then proceeded to use a more direct voice with her, "You better stop this cheating! You know it's wrong. C'mon, get it together."

As a parent, what were my choices? Paisley had done something egregiously wrong and needed to stop immediately. However, she was not happy with herself, had told her teacher *AND* her mom that she had a problem, and she was still trying to figure out how to solve it. As a mom, I wanted to fix it for her, but I felt she had been forthright, and therefore she needed the opportunity to solve her problem.

"I know, I know, I'm just so tempted!" she told me. "I'm going to ask her to do whatever it takes to make sure I can't see anyone else's paper. WHATEVER IT TAKES!"

I knew she had a test the following day. I wanted peek into her classroom to see how she was doing with her problem. The doors had big windows on either side so I had to be very sneaky. Her desk was empty. I scanned the room trying to find her, but I couldn't see her anywhere? *Is she even in here?* Finally, I had to blow my cover. I went in to look for her.

As I walked into the room, I could see the top of my daughter's head. She was sitting on the floor, facing the wall with her work on a clipboard in her lap. My heart welled up. A fourth grader had to be embarrassed by sitting on the floor when all the other kids were at their desks. I walked to the teacher and asked what had happened. She told me that Paisley had chosen to sit on the floor so she wouldn't be tempted to let her eyes wander. Another proud momma moment! She had chosen the right thing to do even if it meant that the other students might tease her. Her integrity was worth more than that. I wasn't frustrated with her anymore. *I admired her.*

But, isn't that lesson true for all of us? Being a Christian doesn't mean we never mess up or get tempted. In fact, we make bad choices all the time. But, we keep trying to get it right. It means we do whatever we need to do to not let sin creep in and cause us to be people that don't honor God. If you are struggling right now with a particular sin, there is hope! Talk about it with your family or friends. Get an accountability partner, no matter how hard or embarrassing that can be. Don't let sin drag you down. Take it to Jesus; He is more powerful than any temptation.

For the Lord gives wisdom; from his mouth come knowledge and understanding. He holds success in store for the upright, he is a shield to those whose walk is blameless, for he guards the course of the just and protects the way of his faithful ones.

—Proverbs 2:6-8

Flood

"When you come out of the storm, you won't be the same person who walked in. That's what this storm's all about."
—Haruki Murakami, Kafka on the Shore

~~~~

ON A SPRING day, a few years ago, a light rain turned heavy within a few hours. The rain was steady, and it continued to rain into the night, and then into the next day. As the second day of rain ended, I was putting Louie, who was a baby, to bed and I noticed that the street looked like it was glowing. *"What is that?"* I thought to myself. When I looked closer, I discovered that the streetlights were reflecting off water flooding the street. *Uh oh, this can't be good.* By the time I went outside to inspect the situation, the water was up to the sidewalk. As I stood there watching, I felt the water begin to touch my toes. It continued to make its way to the house! I knew it could become a serious problem and I could tell my blood pressure was rising.

When we heard that people were evacuating their homes, I asked Michael what he thought we should do. He said that since we had three children, and one of them couldn't swim, then we had better leave for the night. We frantically packed our bags as the water continued to rapidly rise. *Is this really happening? We had never ever flooded before.* Paisley and Eddie were getting nervous because they could see that Michael and I were rushing. We gave them camping bags and told them to pack a couple of outfits and their toothbrush. It was funny to see the things we packed ... especially the kids. We each packed what was important to us: our Bibles, our stuffed teddy bears, and the special binkies (blankets) that we had had since we were babies.

We called our neighbors to see if anyone needed help packing, or getting out of their houses. I saw my neighbors across the street wading through waist deep water to get to our house. *Waist deep! Thirty minutes earlier it was only ankle deep.* I went next door to another neighbor. I found her alone with her daughter; her husband was stuck in the city. I put her daughter on my back and we trudged through the water back to our house. Within 30 minutes, three families had converged in our garage. There we were, five adults, six kids, three dogs and a tiny bird trying to figure out our next move. *How are we going to get out of here? Where will we go once we are on dry land?*

We didn't have much time to think because the water kept rising right before our eyes. We decided to walk or *swim it.* That was really the only way. Michael had our dog in one hand and Paisley in another. I had Louie across my shoulders, and I Eddie by his arm so he wouldn't float away. I am only 5 feet-3 inches (on a good day); when I stepped into that water, it got very deep very fast. We walked. The more I walked the deeper the water got. *Oh my gosh! Paisley's shoes were just swept off her feet!* The water rose to my thighs. *Isn't there an electrical box right around here?* Then it was hitting my hips. The water swirled with debris and whatever else had been in the river's path. Soon it was up to my chest. It was becoming tricky for me to hold the boys and stay upright. *I will NOT let go!* I gripped Eddie tighter as I felt his little body begin to float. *I will NOT let go!* Just when I thought the next step would topple us over and send my boys into an angry river, I began to feel a bit more control and I noticed the water wasn't getting any higher. My footsteps were becoming steadier. Each step brought us closer and closer to dry land. Each step brought us closer to safety. My grip on my son lessened, and I was able to navigate a little easier. As we waded out of the water, we all stared at each other in complete disbelief; we had escaped a flood in our own front yards. We were covered from head to toe in muddy water. We were shoeless and had trash in our hair. But, we had made it.

When I think about that night, I think about all the storms that life brings us. Some of them are real, like the flood, but some of them are circumstances that come our way. We can feel like we are drowning at times, like the water will overtake us at any minute. But, just as I tightly held onto my son in that rushing river, the Lord holds onto you during your storm. He won't let you drown. He will lead you to dry land.

~~~~

For I am the Lord your God who takes hold of your right hand and says to you, Do not fear; I will help you.

—Isaiah 41:13

Shout it

"It's really a wonder that I haven't dropped all my ideals, because they seem so absurd and impossible to carry out. Yet I keep them, because in spite of everything, I still believe that people are really good at heart." —Anne Frank, The Diary of a Young Girl

~~~~

I FELT SHAKEN again. I was on the way to a band competition to watch Paisley, and Eddie had just texted me; there had been a terrorist attack in Paris. *What?* I asked Eddie to make sure that Louie was not watching. We were living in a world of hate and despair. Although my teenager was well aware that true diabolical evil exists, I still wanted to protect my youngest child's innocent heart as long as I could. Judging by the way the world was going, I knew it wouldn't be long.

I found myself fighting back tears in the truck as we made our way down the interstate. I allowed myself to imagine the night in Paris. Any of us could've been there. While innocent people were having dinner and enjoying a night of music and soccer with friends and family, murder and mayhem abounded. However, months before the attack, these innocent victims of terror, these *PEOPLE* were breathing, loving, fearful and wonderful. They were living their lives with hopes and dreams. I'm sure some hoped to fall in love. I bet others yearned for families. To fill their empty arms with children and feel the heartbeat of a newborn with Daddy's eyes. I'm sure some of these people had laughs that could light up a room, or a tenderness about them that could heal even the hardest heart. I bet they could've been our friends. The world will never have the opportunity to know what could have become of them. They are but shadows of those who had walked this place.

It's getting harder and harder to watch the news without being cynical. I struggle with the balancing act between being angry at current events and riding the wave of God's sovereignty. I battle my hatred for those who commit such heinous acts. I have had thoughts that I never thought I would. I never thought I *could* think such bad things. What if that had been Michael? My children? How would I cope? Could I go on in this world with the hope that God is in control. Is our government trustworthy? It all felt topsy-turvy. Right is viewed wrong and wrong is glorified? *Whaaa???* Churches are divided on what the Bible truly says. They add and subtract what they want and call it out-dated. (*Just a side note to that: God maintained the integrity of His word for 2000 years. I think He knows what's best*). I want to scream at the top of my lungs to God and remind Him that although some of our leaders take us down roads that don't glorify Him, not all of us feel that way. Protect us from their mistakes, I pray. I feel like I'm in superglue ... I'm feeling stuck. It makes me anxious all over.

Then, on the other hand, I am reminded of God's promises. How He's got it all together, and He has an order to things. I know the Heavenly Father could make it end right now. He would just have to utter the words and things would be as they should. But, He doesn't. He's not ready yet. There is still more work to be done. He looks down at this hot mess we have made, and He loves every one of His children. Every single one. It's so hard for me to fathom. In this ever-changing world that we live in, our days have been mapped out. He knows what's going to happen, and He has placed us in these times for a reason. Our children have been born exactly when they were supposed to be, and so were we. If we truly believe in the providence of the Lord, we must be willing to be called to do what we need to do at this very time and place. It's been embedded in our DNA.

Looking back through history, we are not the only generation that has faced terrible times. We are not newbies to sin. Consider Herod, the killer of thousands of babies, or the Mayan Indians with pagan sacrifices. Then, more recently, you have Hitler and the Holocaust; millions died. Millions. Currently there is the persecution of Christians and televised beheadings for the world to see. It's barbaric. Evil is not a new concept. Others have gone before us. They have witnessed such atrocities.

I don't know about you, but I have to depend on my faith. There is no other option for me. Satan wants to drown out our joy, but my joy comes flowing from the Father and can't be stolen, quieted, shut down or even killed. I feel the need to forgive. Forgive those who hurt my fellow brothers and sisters. Forgive them for trying to extinguish my faith and love. Forgive them for so many things as I am forgiven for so many things.

I also feel the need to pray. Pray for protection. Pray for our leadership. Pray for the right words and actions that will point people to Jesus during a time that feels like no moral compass exists.

Now is not the time to pretend we can't do anything. We are not called to sit and wring our hands while the world falls apart around us. We are not powerless. We are children of the King. Now is the time to shout the redeeming love of Jesus Christ from the mountaintops, skyscrapers, AND rooftops! People are starving for hope and thirsty for genuine faith. They are craving the Savior. I refuse to walk around in a bitter state, frozen by fear. I will trudge through this mess with the rest of humanity and keep my eyes focused on Him. We have to remember He wins. *His Love wins.*

~~~~

And now these three remain: faith, hope and love. But the greatest of these is love.

—1 Corinthians 13:1

No Matter how Small

"It really boils down to this: that all life is interrelated. We are all caught in an inescapable network of mutuality, tied into a single garment of destiny. Whatever affects one destiny, affects all indirectly." —Martin Luther King, Jr.

~~~~

ONE AFTERNOON, AS I was coming home from teaching, I got stuck in traffic, the kind of traffic where the light turns green, but there isn't enough space for anyone to go through the intersection? The stuff that causes road rage. Well, that was me. It was August, and it was hot. Then, finally, a green light! I thought I would get through!! I inched my way towards the intersection, but NO! Not me! I was stopped, But I would be the first car to go next. So, I sat.

I don't know what you do when you are waiting at an intersection, but when I sit and wait, I people watch. *Hmmm ... what are they doing in their cars? I wonder who they are talking to. Yikes ... those people look mad!* While I was totally zoned out people-watching, a movement caught my left eye. I noticed that one of the electrical poles looked like it was bending. *Huh? How could this be?* Then I saw a very large truck, which I later learned, had jumped the curb while making a turn. And I also realized that the top of the truck had snagged an electrical wire and was in the process of putting a massive amount of tension on it. It kept getting tighter and tighter. And, then, all of the sudden, that huge wooden electrical pole snapped right in half, and down it went. It landed right on a small compact car. It completely crushed it. All of the windows shattered and the doors folded like pieces of paper.

As I watched this unfold, I also heard a strange noise. It sounded like rope being pulled. It was so quick. I looked above me where the stoplights were hanging, and the wires were unthreading right before my eyes. Electrical boxes exploded. *What if it falls on my car?*

I stepped on the gas and drove onto the median where the car had been hit by the pole. *I'm out of harm's way, but what about the person in this car?* I looked around, and no one was going to inspect the car. Some people were on their phones taking pictures, but no one was helping. I called 911 and told them what had happened. Then I decided to make my way over to the car.

I was nervous. *What if the person is dead? What if there is blood everywhere? What if there are children in there?* As I got closer to the car I heard screams. No words, just screams. *At least they are alive.* I had to get on my hands and knees to see inside the car because it was pretty much flattened. *Dear Jesus, I don't know what I'm going to see, but help me do what I need to.*

I looked in and saw a young girl. The poor girl was in shock; she could only scream. Her legs were pinned under the steering wheel, and she was unable to move. I tried to calm her down, but she couldn't hear me over her screams. I looked in the back for a child car seat, but didn't see one. I saw her purse, and I tried to reach it to find identification, but I couldn't get it out. *Why isn't anyone else helping?? I don't know what to do here? I'm just a teacher, not a doctor.* I reached in as far as I could to hold her hand. She noticed my hand, and her tear-streaked face looked my way. She looked right into my eyes, and then quieted.

Just then, a woman came up behind me and told me she was a nurse. I stepped aside. I heard the ambulance coming in the distance. People finally started to arrive at the scene, and I found myself making my way back to my car.

I was totally shaken up. *That was crazy! What just happened? What was my purpose in that whole thing? Why was I there? Why did God stop me at that light?* I felt like I really didn't do anything. I didn't get her free from the car, or even get her name.

But the more I thought about it, I knew I had done something. I may have not done much to help her, but I did *connect* with her, even if for a brief second. Just my being there was enough to quiet her screams. Me, someone who she had never seen before, and would probably never see again.

Think about what life would be like if we took moments, both big and small, to connect with one another. If we embraced any precious opportunity that God gave us to love one another and to let one another know we are not alone.

We are all instruments in each other's lives. We all have a part to play, no matter how small.

~~~~

Do nothing out of selfish ambition or vain conceit. Rather, in humility value others above yourselves, not looking to your own interests but each of you to the interests of the others.

—Philippians 2:3-4

Chair Monster

"You will find peace not by trying to escape your problems, but by confronting them courageously. You will find peace not in denial, but in victory." —*J. Donald Walters*

~~~~

EVER SINCE I can remember I've had a chair in my bedroom. Over the years, the chairs have looked differently. I've had rocking chairs, wicker chairs, and wooden chairs. But, the one thing about the chairs that remained consistent was that they all morphed into *chair monsters*. That's what my parents called them anyway. *You may be thinking, "What is a chair monster?" You probably have one lurking in your room, too.*

A chair monster is a beautiful chair that you can actually sit on in your bedroom. It's useful. It can serve a purpose. But, somehow, this chair becomes home to spare socks, dirty shirts, and maybe that pair of jeans you wore once, but you will wear again before being washed. However, you don't want to take the time to fold and put away just yet. The pile of clothes that sits in the chair becomes so large it can actually take over the room ... hence, the chair monster.

When I was a teenager, my parents constantly told me to clean out the chair monster; it was always the worst job. It meant I would be painstakingly sorting and rehanging clothes for at least an hour. I would always find something in the bottom of the chair, too, a little surprise like a missing shoe or a headband. But, if I got too lazy to really clean it out, I would lay a towel over it. My teenage mind rationalized that if I covered the monster with a towel my parents wouldn't see it. And, if so, they wouldn't make me clean it out. But that never worked.

I had forgotten about the chair monster until the other day when I was folding laundry on my bed. I couldn't find a matching sock, which was nothing new in my family. We usually wore only mismatched socks. I turned around and saw the chair monster in all its glory. And, I started thinking, why do I allow the chair monster to grow? My chair would be so much more useful if I just cleaned it out and put things away where they were supposed to go.

Isn't that just like life?

We all have our own "life" chair monsters, too. When we have issues we don't want to deal with, we often toss them aside. For example, dealing with a disobedient child; we know there is a problem. But we don't feel like arguing so we toss it into 'the chair.' Or that reoccurring issue in our marriage that is never solved because, in order to solve it, we would have to dig deep and go places we might not want to go.

There we go again, another toss.

It could be a problem at work where we may need to confront a co-worker or share the love of Jesus with someone that the Lord is telling us to, but we tell ourselves it's just not worth it, or we don't have time.

Toss, toss!

Then we turn around and we see this massively huge monster that we have created. So, instead of being responsible for it, we sort of handle it by putting a towel over it. We cover it so we don't see the problem. We tell ourselves that life is good; we can work on those things later. We rationalize. However, there is still a giant mess under the towel, which *NEEDS* to be dealt with. And, just like the chair monster makes my bedroom look terrible and dirty, a 'life monster' makes your life messy. At that point, it's time to clean house!

It can be challenging to face problems. Most people do not want to face our part in 'the picture.' We don't want to see what *we* did, or didn't do, to contribute to the monster; if we see it ... then we may have to do the unthinkable and ... *change!* Why is change so scary? If we don't change we don't grow. And if we don't grow, we can't fulfill the purpose the Lord has given us.

If the monster looks too big to handle, take one problem at a time. Don't attack it all at once; save the biggest for last. You may find that most of the issues you were putting aside weren't all that bad. And, even if the problems were difficult, they are not hidden under the towel anymore.

~~~~

Therefore, since we have these promises, dear friends, let us purify ourselves from everything that contaminates body and spirit, perfecting holiness out of reverence for God.

—2 Corinthians 7:1

Life Lesson 4
The Power of Friendship

ALTHOUGH WE ARE stronger than we think, sometimes we just need the love of a true friend ... someone who knows us and accepts us for who we are. We are not designed to handle life by ourselves. We need a support system. We need friends. There's a temptation when we get knocked down to feel ashamed and turn away from the help of others. This is the exact moment when we need our friends most. Pick up the phone and call until a familiar voice and loving heart answers. Turn to friends and they will help you get your bounce back on!

Simply Better

"There is nothing I would not do for those who are really my friends. I have no notion of loving people by halves, it is not my nature." —*Jane Austen,* Northanger Abbey

~~~~

"BLOW OUT THE candles, Eddie!" yell out his friends while holding their cell phones to capture the moment. *Well, it wasn't really a candle because I forgot those on the grocery list. I just stuck a match in the middle of the cake, and they thought that was good enough … sorry Eddie. Mom fail.* But Eddie has been blessed to have an awesome group of friends. In fact, he's had a lot of the same friends for the last decade. It's been so special to see them grow from small, sweet boys to weirdo middle school boys; and then onto high school young men where they get hairy legs and deep voices. I thought this birthday would be the last where we had his buddies over. I mean, 16-year-olds go out to do stuff, but I've still got him when he was 15. When the doorbell had rung, I opened the door and men came in. Every single one of them was taller than me, and I knew they were all shaving … *SHAVING!* But, I enjoyed every second of it! The only problem was that the playroom had become too small for them. It used to fit them better!

Although his friends were all so different from Eddie, they all accepted each other for who they were. A gift they will have forever.

It often amazed me just how we all fit together ... people, I mean. We are all so different. Every person has a different story and a unique background. We all have changing perspectives and changing opinions. We have different dreams and aspirations. But even with our differences, we still need one another.

So many times, we try to handle our lives like we are alone. We take our burdens and worries and hold them close. We are afraid to be vulnerable in front of each other. We act like islands with secure borders surrounded by barbed wire. Why do we spend so much energy acting like we have it together?

Well, this may come as a surprise to some of you, but we are all super messed up ... ***all of us.*** We are sloppy, dirty, difficult, and yes, we are strange. But, the amazing thing is that the Lord has designed and equipped us with these particular gifts, which balance out the weirdness. Think about your friends for a minute. Can you go to different friends for different things? You may go to a certain friend for affirmation or encouragement. You may go to another one for advice or confidentiality. There is always the friend you go to for a great laugh, or, my favorite, the easy friend. That's the friend you can just hang out with, no agenda. Because, if we are honest, not all friends are easy, are they?

Take some time today and appreciate the friends that help you carry burdens, listen to your stories, and love you when you need it the most, or maybe when you don't know you need it. Be thankful for those that challenge you to become a better person and call you out on your nastiness. Be thankful for the ones that you can just look at, a 'you-know-exactly-what-the-other-one-is-thinking' look. Be thankful for the friends that make you laugh so hard your stomach hurts. You know, those people that you can't imagine your days without. Life is simply so much better with friends along the way.

~~~~

Iron sharpens iron, and one man
sharpens another.

—*Proverbs 27:17*

You've Got a Friend

"Is any pleasure on earth as great as a circle of Christian friends by a good fire?" —C.S. Lewis

~~~~

THIS PAST WEEKEND, Michael and I were so grateful to join the wedding celebration of two of our closest friends. Not that all weddings aren't special, but this one was so dear to us because we also saw many other friends we love but normally don't see.

Oh my goodness, it was amazing! The food, you really can't beat wedding food, and the company. I don't know if there is a word that means 'more than a blessing,' but it felt that way. We saw old friends and felt like no time had passed. We were on the dance floor, NOT embarrassing ourselves (that is my perspective, not Michael's), and laughing until we cried. While I was eating my bread pudding I scanned the table and soaked in all the love that was there. I was struck by an overwhelming sense of gratitude to be seated with those who I love and who love me in return. I saw smiles and heard the laughter; and it warmed me body and soul.

My parents were out of town so my children all had to stay at different friend's houses. Have you ever done that? Farm out your kiddos? Sometimes it is necessary. What a gift it was; we had not one, but three different houses where our children felt loved and protected while their parents were gone. Plus, I am blessed by the friendships of those who love my children. It truly does take a village, doesn't it?

The longer I stayed in my cozy, fuzzy place of recognizing my blessings, the more I realized that so many live without knowing the true gift of friendship. We think that friendships are supposed to be easy and fun ... but, not always. I have friends that go back over 20 years, and although we have shared many laughs and wonderful memories, we have also shared heartache that would have been unbearable if we had gone through it alone. Unfortunately, many people are so disconnected with others; they go through these wretched times alone.

We were not created to be alone. We were created to live in community with those around us. It doesn't mean that we will share our deepest longings with everyone, but it does mean we crave real relationships. I guarantee there is someone on your street that is yearning for a listening ear, or there is someone at your grocery store that just wants to be acknowledged with a smile. Reach out to those around you. And, don't always gravitate towards those people who are the easiest to be friends with. Sometimes the most rewarding friendships are those that take the most work. I

challenge you to make a difference in the lives of those
around you, and allow others to bless you in the same way.

~~~~

My command is this: Love each other as I have loved you.
Greater love has no one than this: to lay down one's life for
one's friends.

—*John 15:12-13*

Never Say Never

"There's not a word yet, for old friends who've just met."
—Jim Henson

~~~~

ON THE FIRST day of school, I opened my classroom door, which is decorated with a massive tree made out of colored paper. Hanging from the tree are leaves that have the names of each of my students, my 22 *kindergarten* students. I stepped into the hallway and there they were. I saw those sweet children lined up quietly against the walls. Some of them had blankets or stuffies and were showing them to their new friends. Others were sitting with their backs straight against the wall, eyes staring ahead, afraid of what would happen next. And, of course, there were a few rolling on the floor with their backpacks, picking their noses, totally unaware others were grossed out by their actions.

I became a kindergarten teacher. It was a part-time job, but still a *kindergarten* teacher. Previously, I taught fifth and sixth graders. Many of you might think it would be rather unpleasant to be in a room with eleven or twelve-year-old boys and girls on the edge of puberty. It can be a challenge spending time with the kids that totally smell of B.O. because they haven't started using deodorant yet and whose hormones are completely out of whack. But those are the ones I totally *LOVE* to be with. They challenge me and make me laugh. They are not too old to have fun, but are old enough to take a joke. It's my favorite age.

In fact, I couldn't tell you how many times I have said I would *NEVER* become a kindergarten teacher. Nope, not me. Those kiddos are too young and too needy. They cry a lot, get their feelings hurt, and yes, it must be said, some of them still need help wiping! They put their fingers where they don't belong, and somehow put it on me. I can't tell you how many times I dry-heaved during that year of teaching five and six-year-olds. It was a job share position that I couldn't pass up. My family needed the money, but we still had Louie at home. I didn't want a full time job. Sharing the job meant another teacher and I would switch off; we each worked every other day. It didn't sound *too* bad and it was the only opportunity I had. I know that Jesus was watching me the whole time and laughing at how I had previously said I would *never* do this. *"Yeah, Shannon, we will see about that!"*

Every single day in teaching is totally different. But, in kindergarten every single minute is different. One day, during a small math lesson, I heard a moaning cry come from the cubbies ... where the bathrooms were. I stopped my lesson, and the entire class turned around to see where the cry was coming from. I could see the top of a little boy's head coming from the bathrooms, and I heard him groaning; but I can't see his face through the bookshelves. Not a second later there he was … completely naked, in front of the entire class, screaming at the top of his lungs that he had 'peed on his clothes on accident in the bathroom.' Thus, he refused to put them back on. There I was, standing before this pale, boney, naked little boy while the entire class of five-year-olds screamed and pointed in laughter. I stood there thinking that this was why I thought I would *NEVER* teach kindergarten, but there I was.

Sometimes when life gives you opportunities, they are not exactly what they seem. Yes, I knew this job was not my dream job, and I also knew it was going to be a big challenge changing my teaching techniques to fit into a Kindergarten environment. But, what I didn't know was that my teaching partner would end up becoming a very dear friend. From the hundreds of teachers county-wide, I was partnered with one of the most Christ centered women I have ever known. Not only was she a seasoned kindergarten teacher who allowed me to piggyback on her knowledge (*in fact, she carried me most of the way*), she was my sister-in-Christ and became one of my closest confidants and prayer warriors.

I only taught kindergarten for one year … part-time … and that was about all I could handle. The students did grow on me, and I was able to get into the swing of the routine. But, more than anything, I am forever grateful for the friendship fostered during that time. I'm so happy that Jesus decided to teach me a lesson about what I was *never* going to do, and taught me that His plans are much better than mine. It changed me so much; I rarely say 'never' anymore. Did you get that? I didn't say 'I never say never' because that would be saying *never*!

Think about those things you have said 'never' about. What limitations have you put on yourself? What limitations have you put on *God*? Your 'never' may be the very thing the Lord is challenging you to do. It may be exactly what you need in order to grow in your faith and grow closer to Him. What is it that you are afraid of? What's holding you back? You *never* know, you may end up gaining one of your dearest friends in the process.

~~~

Many are the plans in a person's heart, but it is the Lord's purpose that prevails.

—Proverbs 19:21

Life Lesson 5
The Power of Forgiveness

I CONFESS. IT'S hard for me to say I'm sorry. I'm not the only one who struggles with this. But, asking for forgiveness and giving forgiveness are totally different things. Even if the ones that hurt us don't ask for forgiveness, we are called to give it. But you know what, I've learned that forgiving sets loose God's power in my heart and life. Life's too short to hold grudges. I don't have time for hatred. Neither do you. It will keep you on the ground rather than soaring, where God intended you to be. Being able to bounce back is saying, "I forgive no matter what."

Sorry Seems to be the Hardest Word

"A truly humble apology works to part storm clouds, calm rough seas, and bring on the soft lights of dawn; it has the power to change a person's world." —*Richelle E. Goodrich*

~~~~

A LITTLE WHILE ago, I went through this phase where I was trying to teach Paisley how to cook. It has come glaringly clear that Paisley does NOT like cooking, but I had to try. One day, we had decided to make brownies together. I took this opportunity as a tiny victory! While we were making the brownies, Michael called with some bad news, which left me frustrated and annoyed. It was the type of call that made my blood pressure go from normal to heart attack mode in seconds. When I hung up the phone, I returned to the kitchen to find that Paisley had poured not 1/3 cup of oil into the brownie mix, but *1 AND 1/3 cup* of oil into the mix. The brownie powder was swimming in a pool of vegetable oil.

I snapped. I grabbed the bowl from her, tossed it in the sink, the oil splashing all over the counter. I looked her straight in the eyes and yelled in the nastiest, witchy way possible, "Why didn't you ask? You RUINED it! What's wrong with you?" It was one of those statements you know your kids will tell their therapist one day.

One look from her was all it took. Her little eyes filled with tears, and she didn't say a word. She hung her head and quietly went up the stairs. With the closing of her bedroom door, my heart sank. I wished she would have yelled back at me, or slammed the door. But, this was different. It was a quiet brokenness. I had really hurt her feelings.

I stood at the kitchen counter and tried to convince myself she deserved it. She never measured, she always rushed, she didn't read the directions ... and then I realized; she was just like her mother ... *ME*. My daughter was reflecting her mother. However, I finally realized that I had been the one to squish our little cooking time together, just like a bug on the floor. She hadn't ruined it, I had. So, up the stairs I went.

I found her on her bed sobbing into her pillow. As I sat by her feet, and touched her back, she didn't pull away, or give me the death look. She simply waited for what I had to say.

I really gave it my all. I apologized. It was a good one, too. I admitted to everything I had done, and I did not point out her mistakes. It was a true heartfelt apology, and I meant every word of it. And, she knew it. She embraced me and told me she forgave me. And she also added that she really didn't ever want to cook with me again ... not for a while anyway.

Why is saying "I'm sorry" so hard for some of us. It's like those words seem to get stuck in our throats and refuse to come out. Sometimes, we try to force the words out, you know lasso them and drag them out of our mouths, but, then they can sound harsh and insincere ... almost stabbing. So many times, we dodge saying those 2 little words, and that's what they are ... WORDS! But, think about how different your life could be if you stopped running from the "I'm sorry" and embraced it instead?

Honestly, I'm one of those people who have always struggled with offering a real GENUINE apology. My apologies are always laced with some sort irritating comment, like *Well, I'm sorry that the truth hurts your feelings,* or *Sorry you are hurt by my words, but you've always been sensitive.* But, I'm learning to apologize from the heart. And, of course, my daughter was the one who really taught me.

Looking back, not only did I learn something about a genuine apology, but I also showed my daughter that when you wrong someone, you humble yourself and make it right. How many times, as parents, do we just pass over issues, for which we really should have repented and asked forgiveness? How many times have we yelled at people who weren't driving fast enough for us and our children's ears heard it? How many times have we been at the end of our rope and taken it out on our kids? We don't need to live perfect lives, but we do need to own our issues and our sin, and honor our relationships with our children. If we are to teach them the power and healing behind the apology, and we expect them to do it to others, we need to model it for them ourselves.

~~~~

Get rid of all bitterness, rage and anger, brawling and slander, along with every form of malice. Be kind and compassionate to one another, forgiving each other, just as in Christ God forgave you.

—Ephesians 4:31-32

Just Like a Child

*"Of all your troubles, great and small, the greatest are the
ones that don't happen at all."*
—*Thomas Carlyle*

~~~~

I TOOK PAISLEY to a college night, which was being
offered by the university she wanted to attend. I won't even
get into how I felt … geez! However, Michael was out of
town. So, Eddie, had to be the babysitter for Louie.

Leaving those two together was either a really great idea, or
a really terrible one. Some nights I received a phone call
every five minutes, and other nights I didn't hear a thing.
College night was a good night. They both had homework
to do and other things around the house that kept them
busy. So, all in all, it was a quiet evening with Paisley.

I got home a little after Louie's bedtime, and I went
upstairs to give him his goodnight kisses (I couldn't miss
one of my favorite times of the day!). When I got upstairs, I
saw my littlest sitting up in bed waiting for me.

"Mom," he said in a trembling voice, "I've got to tell you
something *real* bad."

Hummm ... I wondered what it could this be? Maybe he was in a fight with his brother, or maybe he broke something while I was gone. He was fine when I left, but something had changed.

"Ok," I said, "let me have it."

"Well, you know how I had to take a bath tonight?" And, yes, he was supposed to take a bath. Poor thing, being the youngest I always lose track of when he had last taken a bath ... that is, until I smell him!

"Yes, I remember."

"So, Eddie filled up the bath water. When it was done, I jumped in, but I didn't check to see if the water felt good or not. The water was *REALLY* hot."

This is where his lips started to quiver and his voice cracked.

"Go on," I told him.

"When I got in, I said something really *really* bad because the water was so hot. I said Oh my G-O-D (he spelled it out just like that), instead of saying Oh my G-O-S-H. I told Jesus all about it, and He said that He forgave me, but He also said I was supposed to tell you, too."

Oh my heart!! Now, you may not think this is a big deal, but in our house, we don't say Oh My G-O-D. My poor boy had been so anxious all night long because he had said something that he shouldn't have said. He was in knots about it. We talked about what he said. I told him I was sad about it, but I was so honored that he told me. I could tell he was feeling better, and I smothered him with kisses and proceeded to tuck him in when I felt something very strange. He seemed bulky or thick under the covers. I lifted the sheets, and although it was dark, I noticed something didn't look quite right.

"Louie, what's going on with your pjs?" I asked.

"Oh," he said, " I kinda thought you might spank me for saying that, so I put on my undies, two pair of blue jeans and my pj pants on top of that just in case."

Oh my goodness!! What a mess this child was. Didn't he think I would notice that he had on four layers of clothes?

"Are you comfortable like this?" I asked him.

"NO! I'm really hot!"

After he took off his layers, and I tucked him in for real, I thought about his shenanigans and how it's really not that different than how many of us treat the Lord.

When we do something wrong, we might anxiously await some terrible punishment from the Heavens, like being struck by lightning or swallowed up by a massive earth-quake. We can carry around our guilt and prepare for the worst. But, Jesus isn't out to strike us down. He knows there are consequences of sin ... death. But, He also paid a huge price so that we could be alive in Him. He loves us. He is there when we sin, and He is there with open arms when we repent. We don't have to walk around with several layers on *just in case*. We can walk in confidence that we are forgiven.

~~~~

The LORD is a refuge for the oppressed, a stronghold in times of trouble.

—*Psalms 9:9*

Life Lesson 6
The Power of Belief

EVEN IF NOTHING has worked out the way you thought it would; even if life feels like moving from one disaster to another; even if your confidence has hit rock bottom ... I'm still going to shout to you: You gotta believe. Your best days are ahead. God hasn't forgotten you and He holds you in His hands. You are going to make it. Faith is the key to receiving God's unfailing love. I know how easy it is to fall in despair. And we're all going to have moments when we can't seem to muster the belief that our best is yet to come. Faith encourages faith. Bouncing back requires belief that although you may be in a valley, the mountain tops call you.

The Bearer of Bad News

"The bad news is nothing lasts forever, the good news is nothing lasts forever." —J. Cole

~~~~

I COME HOME from a nighttime run to the drug store. I just received a phone call from my ex-husband telling me that he is going to be taken into jail the next morning. It was not a very good conversation … *at all*. We argued. Why? A million reasons, but really that's just what we did during this time of our lives. But, the whole time we were arguing, all I could think about was that when I got home I was going to have to tell our children that he was in jail. How does a parent even do this? I hadn't even known anyone who had gone to jail at this point. How do I communicate this to our 5 and 3 year old? Again, I felt like he had made this massively huge mess, and I'm stuck with the hard work of explaining it to our children and making them sad.

When I got to my parents house, I walked in from downstairs. I watched my feet go from step to step as I could hear my kiddos' laughter fill the house. I must've not looked too good, because when Paisley saw my face she knew something was going on. I took them upstairs where we had made our new little home, and we all sat down on the floor with our legs crossed over each other. We got as comfy as we could get. I looked into their sweet innocent faces. The thought crossed my mind that maybe they don't' really need to know what's going on. I could just kind of skim over this part in their lives, and they wouldn't really know the difference. They don't really see their dad that often anyway. So, it wouldn't be a huge difference in their lives.

But, then I remembered my promise I made to them. At the very beginning of all this yucky-ness, I made them a promise that I would always be honest with them ... even with the hard parts ... *especially with the hard parts*. Something happens to your heart when people you love don't tell you the truth. You feel dumb, and hurt. You also feel like there is something wrong with you that they couldn't trust you with this information. I had become their safe place. It was a responsibility that I did not take lightly. I never wanted them to feel like they couldn't trust my words. I've always handled their hearts with so much care ... *I still do*. I looked into their eyes. I wanted to capture this moment in my memory because they will be changed after this conversation. It will be different after this ... always.

So, this is how it went:

Me: Guys, I've got some bad news to tell you.

Kids: What?!

Me: Well, remember when I told you that daddy did some things that kept him away from us? One of those things was that he took money without asking.

Paisley: Isn't that stealing?

Me: Yes, it is. Do you know what can happen if you steal?

Paisley: Go to jail?

Me. Yes.

Eddie: (on the verge of tears streaming down his face) I thought only bad guys go to jail. How can daddy go to jail?

Oh my soul! This is exactly what I'm talking about. It's so wrong that I have to tell them all the bad news ALL THE TIME! It totally kills me to see their innocence chipped away when I have to tell them the things that he did. No child should have to think about such things. It's just a stark reminder of how we are not promised life to be fair; we are just promised that we are not alone in our struggles.

Both kids are just in tears now. I scoop them up closer and let them just get it all out. Their little whimpers tears at the very core of me. Part of me wants to explode at my ex-husband for creating such heartbreak, the other part of me wants to curl into a little ball and pretend none of it is really happening. Either one of those choices wasn't good ...

Me: Guys, I know we think that bad guys go to jail. But, it's really just people who have made bad choices. Since daddy made a bad choice and broke the law, he has to go and think about that in jail. It's like his very own long time out.

Paisley: Will we ever get to talk to him?

Me: Yes, he can call us and write you letters, too.

Paisley: (crinkling her little forehead, and looking up with those teary brown eyes) If daddy makes bad choices, does that mean I will too?

You never know when the kids are going to throw a curve ball, and here one was. It never even entered my brain that my ex-husband is an extension of my kids. I'm sure there are parts of him that the kids admire. So, poor Paisley now thinks that since he made those terrible choices, that she is destined to make the same ones.

Me: Nope! Of course not, Paisley! Jesus made us all our own individual selves. Daddy made daddy's choices, and Paisley makes Paisley choices. Just like I make my own choices, too. We all have the opportunity to make good or bad choices everyday.

That answer seemed to satisfy her question. I could feel her small tense body relax a bit. I held those babies as long as they wanted, and then the silence was broken by Eddie wanting to watch T.V. He's always been good at breaking the silence ... *still is!*

I had a lot of difficult days throughout this divorce journey, but that was one of the hardest. I couldn't protect them from that. They needed to know. We tend to underestimate our kids resiliency. Sometimes we handle them like they are made of glass. But, they will totally surprise you. They are truly able to roll with the punches as long as they know we will be by their side guiding them through the process.

The Lord was with me when I was talking to my children that day. He was there every day before, and every day since. But, just as my children look to me for direction, we are meant to look to Him for ours. He will never lead you down the wrong path. All we have to do is trust that He's got us.

~~~~

Blessed is the man who remains steadfast under trial, for when he has stood the test he will receive the crown of life, which God has promised to those who love him.

—James 1:12

Moments

"Should you shield the canyons from the windstorms you would never see the true beauty of their carvings." — *Elisabeth Kubler-Ross*

~~~~

UGH! THIS LIFE didn't look good. As my children slept in their beds, they were completely unaware that I was stressing out. I had just found out I was getting divorced, and I didn't have a job. Plus, I didn't have a college education. Needless to say, my choices were few in the job arena. I constantly looked through the classifieds to find a miracle job, which might accept me with only a high school diploma as well as allow me to have a flexible schedule, maybe even work from home. And, of course, I was looking for a job with a six-figure salary. I knew those kind of jobs didn't exist. It was becoming glaringly clear; if I didn't want to work numerous small jobs to make ends meet, I was going to have to get my degree. Geez! At the time, anything else would have seemed better than that. I had never been the best student, but mostly because I was too social. I did have a 'lost' semester in college right out of high school, but it's called the lost semester for a reason. The actual problem, however, was that I didn't love school.

When I thought about going back, I knew I'd be the old one. The single mom divorcée with two kids taking English 101. Yep, that would be me!

Returning to college was a completely different experience, though. This time I had a goal. I wasn't there to meet new people, or even have a good time. I was there to acquire skills that would, in turn, give my children opportunities. I took as many classes as allowed each semester, and I went through the summers, too. Most days, I was awake before the sunrise, and after I put the children to bed I was worked on homework. There were times I was invited out and I couldn't go, or I had to miss something at the kids' school because I was taking classes. Often, the children wanted attention, and I had a deadline for a project or paper; I felt torn in a million different directions. It was an incredibly difficult time. However, I kept that goal in the forefront of my mind. It took three years of pure dedication, determination, and a lot of sacrifice.

Finally, one cold, but sunny day in December, I woke early. It was the day I had been working for those few years. I drove myself to the college and dressed in my cap and gown. I looked at my reflection in the mirror. I knew my own reflection, yet I looked so different. My eyes told a new kind of story, one that hadn't before been told. I thought, *"Is this really happening? Is this really me?"* Right about then, I heard the call to line up. I kept glancing around the stadium looking for my family. But, all I could see was an ocean of blurry faces. I just wanted to find them ... see them. I couldn't have taken this journey without them, and I needed to share this moment with them.

When my name was called, I still couldn't believe that *my* name was on the graduation list! I walked across the stage with my head high. I offered an outstretched hand to receive that piece of paper I had worked so hard for. It was my time. As I walked down the stairs, I heard "Mom!" I looked up and there they were ... my children, my parents, my family ... And then came the tears. All of us. My children were worth all that sacrifice. *I* was worth it. It was one of those life-changing moments, which I will remember for all time. The moment I learned what real honor felt like. The moment when I realized that perseverance really could bring forth character. I had kept that goal in my mind, but really it was the road that took me there where I learned the most.

Life is made up of moments that design and create the people we are. Some of those moments are out of our control like death, tragedy, or even winning the lottery. But, some of those moments are of our own making. Graduating college was one of my moments. If you are faced with a challenge or obstacle right now, no matter how big it may seem, know that with God's help it is truly possible to overcome. He will never give you anything you can't handle; He wants to see you succeed. Sometimes, you just have to take that first step.

~~~~

Being confident of this, that he who began a good work in you will carry it on to completion until the day of Christ Jesus.

—Philippians 1:6

My Best Friend's Wedding

As my sufferings mounted I soon realized that there were two ways in which I could respond to my situation -- either to react with bitterness or seek to transform the suffering into a creative force. I decided to follow the latter course."
—Martin Luther King, Jr.

~~~~

I HUNG UP the phone with my best friend's boyfriend. Sounds like a totally weird sentence, but it did have a good purpose. We had never talked on the phone before, but he was calling to invite my husband and me to a party he was planning. He was in the process of designing a clever proposal plan, and after she said, "Yes!" he wanted to bring her back to his house, which would be full of all their closest friends for a grand celebration. Oh my gosh! There is no way to describe how excited I was for her. She had waited for just the right one, and we all absolutely loved him. He was perfect for her, and she was swimming in happiness.

Little did they know, or did *I* know, my husband and I were going to separate just a couple of months after their engagement. I knew we were not in a good place, but when they threw the party, he was still up for making it *look* like we were sort of happy. So, we went. I was so happy I was there to see them walk through the door, my friend with her man by her side and that beautiful diamond ring on her finger! The smile on her face showed true joy, and she really did glow with love and anticipation of the future with her new fiancé.

Coming home from the party, reality set in again. The dark heaviness of my marriage snuck back into my life, and I began to crumble under the weight. I was all smiles leaving the party, but all tears when we got home. It was so good to have my mind focused on my best friend and all her happiness. It felt like home to be able to laugh and feel lighthearted. I really started to see what kind of person I had become living with such stress for so long. I had lost a lot of my joy.

Several weeks after that party, I had to call my friend and give her some news I didn't want to tell her, but that I *had* to tell her. She needed to know my husband and I were going through some major troubles, and I had asked him to leave. I *so* didn't want to tell her those things, but it was necessary for her to know. She is like family to me; and besides, she would be able to sense it, anyway.

She was very understanding, as she has always been. She suggested I not do any of the wedding activities with her; she knew it could be hurtful to watch her get married while my own marriage was ending. Although I knew she would say that, I already knew that I wouldn't miss being a part of this season in her life for anything ... not even my own divorce. We had prayed for her husband, and had waited for him to come into her life. I wouldn't let my own problems keep me from celebrating her. I didn't know just how good that decision would be for me.

Because of her wedding, I was able to forget my problems, even if it was just for a few hours here and there. It allowed my brain a vacation from the dark places and allowed me to focus on the good things like friendship, love, and the beginning of something wonderful. Being able to witness her merging her life with her husband was a gift God knew I needed at exactly that time.

Although my world was filled with divorce lawyers, children, and moving boxes, it was also filled with bridal showers, long lasting friendships, and happy tears. It was truly a relief to get my mind off of my own issues and pour myself into my friend's joy. Self-pity is truly destructive.

It wasn't easy all the time. My heart ached when I saw the other girls in the bridal party with their husbands, and mine ... well, mine was a felon. My friend's wedding helped me begin to bounce back from my divorce ... even in the smallest of ways. There is no better medicine for the soul than giving to others when you are having a difficult time.

On a cold day in December, my best friend got married. I was honored to stand beside her as they made their promises to one another. I was there to witness one of the most important days of her life because she was one of the most important people to me. And although I didn't get to dance with my own husband at the reception, I did dance with two of the most amazing children on the planet. It was a good, *good* day!

The valleys in life don't ever ask permission when to make their entrance. They just come at their leisure. But, when we turn our focus inward and become self-absorbed we forget about the life that is happening all around us because we are blind. We become jealous and bitter. God's design for us is to not fall victim to life's downfalls, but to overcome these things with love. If you are in a "low" right now, take heart. It's just a season. But, if all you do is dwell on the negative, it can become a lifestyle. Instead, invest in those around you. Happiness is contagious. Don't miss out on the forever good because of the temporary bad.

~~~~

Rejoice with those who rejoice; mourn with those who mourn.

—Romans 12:15

Here's What I'd Do

"We spend the first twelve months of our children's lives teaching them to walk and talk. And, we spend the next twelve telling them to sit down and shut up." —Phyllis Diller

~~~~

ONE NIGHT, PAISLEY asked me to come into her room for one of our late night talks. I was so tired and just about ready to get all snuggled up, and she said, "Mom, can we talk?" Well, of course, you know I talked. As she discussed whatever was on her teenage heart, I decided to not offer up any help. I was just going to listen and see what she had to say. When she talked, I asked questions and was genuinely interested. But, when she was done talking, I hugged her and got up to leave. She stopped me. "Wait! So, you are not going to tell me what to do?" I looked back at her, "Nope. Not this time. I think you got this." And before my very eyes, I saw my daughter gain so much confidence from that one sentence. I knew she was capable. I knew she was responsible and kind. I believed in her, and the most important part was that she knew it.

But it hadn't always been this way: I am a recovering advice giver!

I love talking to ALL people about their problems ... not just my children. I don't know what it is, but I just love it when people are their true authentic selves and are vulnerable enough to share something they are struggling with. I like talking about *my* issues, too! Not to the point where I don't talk about anything else; I often needed someone else's insight on how to handle a problem. However I enjoy the give and take relationship, which is possible when sharing each other's burdens.

I liked to hear about others struggles, and I liked to give advice ... even when I was not asked for it. Sometimes people want to be heard, and they aren't ready to figure it out. But, for some reason I went that extra step and tried to help others solve their problems.

Exhibit A: All of my children.

When children are little, we get used to making decisions for them. You know: which shoes to wear, bacon or sausage, milk or orange juice. But the older they get, they do this really ridiculous thing and start making choices for themselves. The problem arose when I still thought *I* should be making their choices for them. That became harder when the teenage years arrived.

One always hears stories about how teenagers are unpredictable and crazy. Part of that is true, but not all of it. I love raising my teens. I was super blessed that both of the teenagers talk to me; they really *talk* to me. Of course, Paisley talks way more than Eddie. But, when they came to me with a problem, I would always (not sometimes, not every now and then, but ALWAYS) say, "Well, *I* would blah, blah, blah." I always offered advice. It didn't matter if they asked for my help or not, I would just spit it out. And, most of the time they would take it, and it worked out fine … until they started thinking for *themselves!*

It stopped working when they started high school. I started getting rolling eyes and heavy sighs. "Mom! Listen to what I'm saying! I'm not asking for help. I just want to tell you what happened*!" Ummm … what? Really? You DON'T want me to tell you how to fix it? Why wouldn't you? I have the answer right here!! It's perfect! Just let me tell you!* I would stare into their eyes, I could see their lips moving, but I wouldn't really be listening. All I could do was think about how they didn't want to hear what I had to say.

By always offering my advice, I had undermined my children's abilities. They were not making their *own* decisions; they were living out *my* decisions. So, in reality, they couldn't be as rewarded by the successes, and they couldn't learn as much from the failures. I hadn't allowed them to trust in themselves. I had subconsciously taken that away.

I had to remember that Jesus loved my children. He loved them way more than I ever could. That didn't mean I didn't parent them; it just meant that if I was telling my children to put their faith in Jesus, I had to be able to do the same.

~~~~

All Scripture is God-breathed and is useful for teaching, rebuking, correcting and training in righteousness, so that the servant of God[a] may be thoroughly equipped for every good work.

—2 Timothy 16:17

Bumpy Ride

"Never be afraid to trust an unknown future to a known God." —Corrie Ten Boom

~~~~

I WAS STARVING to death! I was so hungry, I could have eaten anything … and I meant anything. I had spent the entire day drinking only clear liquids, and having the occasional banana popsicle and half a bowl of orange Jello. I found myself imagining I had just eaten the juiciest steak along with a steaming hot baked potato covered in melted butter running down the sides. I pretended I was full to the brim with deliciousness. But, it didn't work. I knew my belly was totally empty and craving just the smallest saltine cracker. But, I had to deny, deny, and deny once more. Blah!

This was NOT normal for me, but it was doctor's orders. I was having some tests done, and it was part of the whole prep thing. The prep was AWFUL. I REALLY liked food, but I had been having some stomach issues. It was time to get checked out. I had suffered from stomach issues my entire life, but they had gotten worse as I got older.

If I were to be completely and utterly transparent, I was scared. The procedure didn't make me nervous, just the results. *What if they are life changing? What if they find something that can't be treated? What if they do? What if they don't find anything at all? Then what?*

Of course, me being me, I did the most terrible thing one could possibly do when having medical issues. I looked online and searched my symptoms. Why did I do this to myself? All I saw were things that were awful. But what was I looking for? I was looking for an article would tell me I would be okay. But, of course, no such article existed. The only articles I found told me about the worst case scenario. *I should start counting my days, and getting my affairs in order. Ok ... now that's being a little over dramatic I confess, but that's how it felt!* To make matters worse, I had done the research late at night, in bed, right before I went to sleep. *I could think about it all ... night ... long ...*

All the "*What If*" questions filled my mind. I was allowing my deepest and darkest feelings to emerge. They can wrap around even the strongest of people and choke out faith if we allow them to. I allowed images of my family to fill my mind ... the worst of the worst. I allowed myself the thought of my children growing up without me around. *What would that look like? What if I couldn't see them graduate or get married? What if I never witnessed them as parents? How could they handle it? What would my husband do? How would this change his life?* Before I knew it, I was crying silent tears (so I wouldn't wake Michael who was sleeping next to me). I knew I was being foolish for traveling down that road. I knew it really wasn't healthy, but I couldn't help it.

Eventually, I decided I didn't like visiting that place of sadness. It made me feel terrible and full of angst. Did it change anything? Did it help the situation at all? No! All it did was take my eyes off of Jesus, and it also stole my hope. I had been totally psyched out by that I'm sure the Lord was thinking, "Shannon, why have you done this to yourself? Take it easy."

So, I decided to pray. I prayed for my body. I prayed for my health. I prayed for my attitude. I prayed for the ability to accept the outcome ... no matter what. The 'no matter what' part was the key to *that* prayer. And, then I said a prayer of gratefulness. Grateful for what I had been given, and grateful I had a Heavenly father who had my back.

I started thinking about Jesus walking on the water when Peter wanted to meet him. Peter had faith. He got out of the boat and began to walk on the water. But, just like life, the wind picked up, Peter got scared, and then started to sink. But, here's the part I have always liked. Jesus didn't pluck Peter from the water with a wave of his hand and magically float him back to safety. He didn't even make the wind stop until they had climbed back into the boat. He walked to Peter, met him where he was sinking, and then reached out to him to save him.

It made me think about my situation. I was in a storm. The wind was picking up, and I was getting nervous. Although

Jesus had the authority to quiet the storm, He didn't. Instead He met me in my storm and helped me through it. He always will. If Jesus always took the storm away, we would never learn from it. And, we wouldn't need to depend on Him.

If there is a storm in your life, depend on Jesus. Call upon His name. Loving Jesus doesn't guarantee smooth sailing; there will be bumpy rides. But, He promises to meet you where you are and help you as you navigate your way.

~~~~

Now faith is confidence in what we hope for and assurance about what we do not see.

—Hebrews 11:1

New Horizons

"Moving on is a simple thing, what it leaves behind is hard." —Dave Mustaine

~~~~

WHEN I WAS 15, I had to move from the only city I had ever lived in to a brand new place. I was leaving behind my home, the one church I had ever been part of, and tons of family and friends. Up until that point, my life had been very familiar and comfortable. Suddenly, I was going to a place where I didn't know anyone, and I was really nervous about what the future would hold.

I remember the first day of school. It was so different. I didn't know where anything was; it took me forever to get to my classroom. I didn't recognize anyone's face, or name, and they didn't know mine. I was walking through the hallways among strangers, and I felt so *alone.*

It wasn't that I didn't know anyone here; it was so very different from my previous school. I had grown up in a city. My old high school was surrounded by cars honking and sizable buildings. There were a lot more students at my old school and it was always a struggle just to get through the halls. Not only was it crowded, but it was physically big, too … like a small college campus.

But the new school was really different. It was surrounded by fields and cows. The only building I could see was the middle school directly across the street and a random house here and there. The school was so small; and it felt like most of the students had known each other since conception!

Feeling lonely toward the middle of the day, I searched through my purse and prayed I could find a quarter to use the pay phone to call my mom. *Yes! Found one! Please be home, please be home! Yes!* She picked up and I told her she needed to come and get me because I felt like a complete outsider. I was covering the receiver like I was an FBI undercover agent. I couldn't let anyone hear what I was saying. Of course, she didn't come and whisk me away to home school dreamland. She told me to stick it out, and it would all end up ok. In the words of DJ Jazzy Jeff and the Fresh Prince, *"Parents just don't understand."*

Luckily for me, she was right. It wasn't too much longer before I met some girls that ended up becoming my closest friends. The type of friends that you can tell anything to and not feel judged … only loved. We were not just friends in high school, but we remained lifelong friends. Our friendship has lasted through marriages, moves, baby births, divorces, sicknesses, and even funerals. We have changed together, cried together, and prayed together. My children have never known life without them. But, through it all, our friendship has remained as strong as ever.

What a gift God gave me. During a time when I was only thinking about what I was leaving behind, He had such wonderful things laid out before me. If you are in a season of change, which can be scary, remember that The Lord has plans for you, which are going to be better than anything you can imagine.

~~~~

Therefore I tell you, do not worry about your life, what you will eat or drink; or about your body, what you will wear. Is not life more than food, and the body more than clothes?
—Matthew 6:25

Life Lesson 7
The Power of Time

MY STORY WILL be just one voice of encouragement you hear on the journey of bouncing back. Be patient with yourself. Give yourself time to grieve and heal from whatever has happened to you. Just be aware that one step at a time, God is renewing you inside and out into the woman He made you to be—your best you ever.

Never Alone

"The most terrible poverty is loneliness and the feeling of being unloved." —Mother Teresa

~~~~

HUMANS ARE MADE to live in community. We just are. Some crave that community more than others. I enjoy small groups of people, but I can get overwhelmed easily with too many conversations. Normally I retreat to a corner somewhere and chat with the same person all night long. It's just how I'm wired.

But, there is a tremendous difference between being an introvert and being lonely. I have truly been lonely and it is a miserable feeling.

The year my ex-husband and I separated, before our divorce was finalized, I had to face the holiday season alone. Halloween was right around the corner, then came Thanksgiving, and, of course, Christmas was soon after. On top of figuring out my totally crazy and bizarre personal life, I also had to continue to celebrate these times for my kids' sake. I had *so* wished we could've skipped these; my brain was having enough difficulty getting through each regular day, not to mention a holiday!

Halloween and Thanksgiving weren't too horrible. I was packing up our home, and we were moving in with my parents; plus I was navigating Paisley who was four years old and Eddie who was two years old through the hardest time in their little lives. Although we were in a chaotic season, my mind was occupied with details. I couldn't focus on how I was really *feeling* about being alone ... until Christmas came.

When Christmas came, I struggled. It was the first time I had allowed my heart to feel the absence of 'what once was.' Everywhere I looked, people seemed to be floating on a cloud of sheer Christmas joy. There was love and anticipation of the season in the air. Children were trying to be on their best behavior, and parents were the secret keepers.

On the other hand, I was selling off furniture, talking to divorce lawyers, and feeling very much alone. I remember thinking 'I'm going to take a family picture this year. We do it every year, and this year will be no different.' But, when I saw the picture, it was really just a glaring reminder that my family was *broken* ... along with my heart.

I was lonely. Not the kind of lonely where you don't have anyone around, but the kind of lonely where there are tons of people around and you *still* feel desolate. It was like a part of me had been amputated. Although it was gone, I could still somehow feel it. I would try to put on a good face, but the authentic part of me would remind me that I was, indeed, by myself.

But something changed on Christmas morning. I promise I'm not being cheesy, but I had a complete change of heart on Christmas day. My children woke up that morning like many other children...ready to attack the presents. By the time I rolled out of my bed and walked to our little Christmas tree, the kids were jumping up and down. Paisley was flapping her little hands, which she always did when she was excited, and Eddie was just randomly squealing. It was the smiles that caught my attention. Since the divorce had started, I could not remember their smiles being quite as beautiful as on that Christmas morning.

After all the presents were freed from their shiny wrappings, my babies climbed into my lap and snuggled. They didn't say anything; they were tired from all the excitement, but I could hear Eddie sucking his thumb and Paisley was curling my hair around her finger. And, I knew, *I wasn't alone after all.* My husband had left our family, but my Savior had not. My children were with me body and soul. They were healthy and loved. He had allowed me to have the most precious gift that Christmas morning ... the gift of perspective. Just because my family looked different than it used to, it didn't mean it wasn't still my family. I had hands to hold, bodies to hug, and cheeks to kiss goodnight. I was overwhelmingly blessed.

Loneliness affects us all at different times in our lives, and different situations stir up lonely feelings. You may think about how you don't have that family you want and/or that your life has been harder than others. That very well may be the case. But you do have the opportunity to create family by pouring into your friends and the less fortunate around you. If you are feeling lonely, try not to focus on what it is that you *don't* have. But, put your eyes on the Lord, and on the gifts He has *given* you.

~~~~

A father to the fatherless, a defender of widows, is God in his holy dwelling. God sets the lonely in families, he leads out the prisoners with singing; but the rebellious live in a sun-scorched land.

—Psalm 68:5-6

Sticks and Stones

"I have hated words and I have loved them, and I hope I have made them right." —*Markus Zusak*, The Book Thief

~~~~

WHY DO YOU feel the need to leave every night? Why don't you want to stay around and be with me? I remember asking my ex-husband these questions shortly before my little world fell apart with my divorce. He had made a habit of leaving every night. I never knew where he was going, when he was coming back, or even *IF* he was coming back. Our chaotic life had become my new normal. His answer to me is one I will never forget. Even after all these years I can still see his face while saying these words, *"You don't bring joy to anyone. I see no value in you, and no one does."* It was like being punched in the gut.

Sticks and stones can break my bones, but words can never hurt me. How many times have we heard this saying? How many times have we repeated it to ourselves between crying eyes and sobs? Whoever wrote that must've had a complete disconnect with the real world. Words can really, *really* hurt us. They have so much power in them. I mean, think about it?? Can you remember all the people who have told you how much you are loved? I'm sure names and faces of parents, siblings, kids, grandparents, friends, and neighbors all pop up in your mind. But, do you think you could name them all? Probably not. There are too many.

But, what if I asked you to think about the people who hurt you with words? Maybe they told you they hated you, or insulted you. That list is probably much shorter. I know exactly who has wounded me over the years. If I think about who has hurt me with their words, the list is short, but the impact was astounding.

After my divorce, I felt like a huge nothing. I had been worn down to a tiny emotional stub. My ex-husband fought many demons, and many times I was the brunt of his anger and frustration. The words my ex-husband spoke were like chains around my neck. Every jab was another link. The weight became unbearable. So much so, I remember physically walking like I was carrying invisible pounds on my back. My head would hang down, and my shoulders would slump. I thought he didn't want to be around me because I wasn't pretty enough, witty enough, attentive enough … well, I guess I thought he didn't want to be around because I just wasn't enough in general. As a wife, that can totally do a number on your head!

I remember once having a moment to myself, and reading my *People* magazine. This particular issue had an article about celebrity marriages that had failed. Many of them had failed because of adultery and betrayal. I distinctly remember looking at all of the wives with husbands that had strayed. Here they were. Beautiful: size two, no gray hairs, and if they had any wrinkles, I couldn't see them. They were Hollywood glamor personified! I thought: These women had it all, and yet, they were still not immune to 'not being enough.'

I had one of those "a-ha" moments. We aren't created to be enough. We are not supposed to be enough. We aren't meant to complete another person. That is Jesus's job, not ours. My ex-husband had put me in the position to make him happy. He had made it my responsibility to make him feel certain ways. He had put his trust in an imperfect person ... me. And, I had let him down because there was no way I could live up to that expectation. But, you know what? I had done the same thing. I had allowed my situation to turn my eyes away from Jesus. I had allowed someone to speak lies to me, and I had come to believe them. I let myself find my worth in my ex-husband, not in my Creator. And, none of it was working.

It took a long time for me to recover from that. Every time the poisonous words would seep from my memory, I would literally have to pray them away. I had to make a habit of speaking words of truth to myself. I wasn't going to allow Satan to rob me of my dignity. It just wasn't me that was at stake, I also had two children at the time that needed me to be strong and healthy for them. After a while, I began to notice I was able to stand a little taller. The links were slowly disappearing from my chain. I had become free. I was beginning see shimmers of my spirit bouncing back.

All of us have a choice in how we use our words. We can all be curt sometimes and say things we don't mean. But we don't ever want our words to permanently scar someone's spirit. We can either speak the love of Christ in truth to one another, or we can break someone's spirit with our hateful speech and insults. Which one are you going to be?

~~~~

A good man brings good things out of the good stored up in his heart, and an evil man brings evil things out of the evil stored up in his heart. For the mouth speaks what the heart is full of.

—Luke 6:45

The Necklace

"In three words I can sum up everything I've learned about life: it goes on." —Robert Frost

~~~~

WE ARE ALMOST there! My sister and I raise our hands as our parents go faster and faster over the little hills that lead to my Nonna and Poppy's house in Arkansas. It's like our very own personal roller coaster ride, which we get to go on every time we visit. Our stomachs would end up in our throats, and we would fill the car with little girl laughter.

What seemed like forever was simply a few hours; We would pull into the gravel driveway at their house, which we lovingly called "The Farm." It was one of the most beautiful houses I had ever seen, and it was the most awesome grandparent house. There was glitter sprinkled on the ceiling, which I pretended was stars when I would fall asleep. They had a massively huge garden that we could play in and a couple of barns to explore, as well. They even had a creepy room next to the stairs, which was the perfect threat if we ever decided to misbehave.

Nonna and Poppy were sweet, loving people that had grown old together. Being at their house always included special treats like midnight snacks and creamy, sugar sweet coffee (which my mother never wanted us to drink ... geez ... I wonder why). My grandmother always wore a heart shaped diamond necklace, which my grandfather had given her for their 25th wedding anniversary. The necklace was not big and gaudy, but simple and sweet. Whenever I would snuggle up in her lap, I would twirl it around my finger and look at it sparkle. She wore it as a reminder of their love and devotion to each other.

As the years passed and I grew, my grandparents also got older. As life does, it gives and it takes away. My grandmother went on to 'glory' as she called it. I was overwhelmingly honored to find that she had left me her heart shaped necklace, which she had loved so much. Although I don't have my Nonna on this earth anymore, I still have a precious reminder of her. I decided I would wear the necklace every Easter because it reminds me that one day I will see my grandmother again. I also wear it every Mother's day to remember the love my grandmother showed me. When I wore it, it laid close to my heart just as she was close to my heart. It is truly an heirloom.

Recently, though, someone came into my home and stole my grandmother's necklace. They plucked it out of its hiding place, and now it's gone ... forever. It shattered my heart into tiny pieces. It wasn't like some sort of natural disaster had blown our house off its foundation and we had lost all our valuables. Someone who had bad intentions decided something of ours looked valuable and took it for themselves. Someone who didn't know and who didn't care about what that necklace meant to me stuffed it in his pocket. I'm sure he didn't know of my plans to give it to my own daughter someday so she would have a piece of her great-grandmother close to her, as well. I'm sure he didn't recognize the fact that it wasn't just a necklace to me ... it was a memory. Of course, we did all we could do to recover it. However, the odds of getting back stolen jewelry are so very slim. *How could someone do this to me? How could someone just come into my home and take something that is so very dear?*

At first, I was overwhelmed with sadness and anger. So many memories flooded my mind...the farm, the piano playing, the smell of my Nonna's coconut lotion. The little necklace that meant so much to me was gone. This reminder of a loving marriage and Godly legacy ... stolen. I thought of all the times I had run my fingers over it and examined it as I sat on my grandmother's lap. I thought of how I would lay my head on her chest and hear her heart beat.

The more I thought about it, though, the more I realized that although the necklace had so much sentimental meaning, it was really just a necklace. My *grandmother* is what made it special. My Nonna, who taught me the love of hymns, and showed us off by having us sing in front of the church. She gave me childhood memories on the farm with my cousins; she had taught me how to make an apple pie with just the right amount of cinnamon and sugar. She had taught me the importance of family. She had told me that all the answers I would ever need are in the Bible. All of these things could never be taken away because they were safe inside my heart. They had been imprinted on my spirit. It's part of who I am ... my DNA. *That's* her legacy, and that's the *real* heirloom.

~~~~

But from everlasting to everlasting the Lord's love is with those who fear him, and his righteousness with their children's children.

—Psalms 103:17

Loss

"Grief does not change you, Hazel. It reveals you." —*John Green*, The Fault in Our Stars

~~~~

I GRIMACED IN my sleep. My eyes opened immediately. I was in so much pain, the kind of pain that causes a cold sweat. I got out of bed. It was four AM in the morning. *Why does this kind of stuff always happen at the most ungodly hours?* I couldn't even stand up straight. I looked over at Michael sleeping. I hated to wake him. We were in the midst of a wonderful family vacation in Florida. At that point, we still had a couple more days to go. *Maybe if I lay on my belly the pain will go away. Nope, that doesn't work.* Nothing I did worked. The pain was so sharp and showed no sign of easing.

Geez, it's probably my appendix. Where is my appendix? Is it on the right or left side? Well, I knew something had to be done because no matter what I did, the pain was not going away. It was a stabbing, sharp, throbbing kind of pain, and I knew the sooner I could get it to go away the better. I rolled over and lightly tapped Michael. Well, at least I thought I had tapped him. I must've punched him because he sat straight up in bed. *"What's the matter?"*

I told him I needed to go to the emergency room. He looked nervous. We hadn't been married a year, and it had been quite a year. We had moved … twice, blended a family, and were expecting our first baby. We hadn't wasted any time. I was used to a chaotic life of children and uncertainty. But, poor man, I didn't think he could handle too much more.

We woke my parents who were vacationing with us. They assured us they could handle everything with Paisley and Eddie. So, we made our way to the hospital. The whole time we were driving I'm thinking, well, what could it be? By that time, I had decided the shrimp and grits that I had eaten the previous night was the cause. They were probably rancid. That's it.

We finally arrived to the hospital, and we went through the full admittance whole process: You know, name, date of birth, recent surgeries, three months pregnant. They admitted me and gave me the most amazing thing: morphine. Ahhhh … relief. Thank Jesus for pain relievers. Good thing they didn't give me a drip or I would've been pressing that button all night long.

They took blood and ran tests. Of course, I was worried about the little baby. An ultrasound before we had left for vacation revealed a perfect baby … heartbeat and all. *If it's my appendix can they operate even though I'm pregnant?*

A young doctor arrived. He looked very official for someone so young. He had a clipboard in his hand, wore a white coat, and even had extra pens in his pocket. He proceeded to tell us that all the tests looked good. *Well, that's news I like to hear! But, what could it be?* Then he gave me his medical opinion: "This is a bad case of ... gas." *Wait. What the what? Did he just say I have a bad case of gas?* I was in a tizzy! I wanted to know where he had gone to school. *Did he put 50 bucks in the mail and got a medical degree in return?? GAS?* I'd had gas before. In fact, I'd had gas a lot, trust me, this was not gas. Michael looked at me with that *"are you kidding me?"* look.

When we left the emergency room, I still could not stand up straight because the pain was so bad. It was ludicrous; I knew I had to return home to my real doctor. We went back to the vacation house and packed up our things. My children were worried, but they were with my parents. They would stay and finish their vacation while Michael and I started for home. We knew we wouldn't make it in time to see the doctor that day, but we had an appointment first thing in the next morning.

The next morning I got ready for the appointment. The sharp pain had become a dull soreness. It wasn't too bad, but I still wanted to be checked out. When we arrived at the doctor's office, the first thing they did was send me for an ultrasound. I turned towards the black screen to watch it light up to see the little baby. But I didn't see anything. *Uh oh ... this can't be good.* The technician left the room and brought back the doctor to see me. The doctor kept telling me to lie down, but I didn't feel like lying down. I just wanted to know what was going on. She took my blood pressure: 70/20. *What? How can that be?? What is happening?* She explained to my husband and me that I needed to be rushed into surgery for a ruptured ectopic pregnancy. *Huh? We just saw the baby last week. It wasn't a tubal pregnancy.* The doctor then further explained that I was carrying twins. One was tubal and the other one was not. But, the rupture had caused me to bleed internally and the other baby did not survive. *What are the chances? Well, it's actually one in 30,000 pregnancies if you really want to know.*

She told me to go directly to the hospital and she would meet me there to perform the surgery. Without it, she said, I would die. Oh my gosh ... this was really serious! My life became a blur. They didn't even admit me to the hospital. They wheeled me directly to surgery prep. Someone handed me a sharpie and I wrote my name and birthdate on my arm ... just in case. I didn't want to wake up to a missing leg amputated or have surgery meant for someone else. The last thing I remember is Michael holding my purse while they whisked me away to save my life. He looked so small standing in that huge doorway.

It took me a while to come to grips with the loss. The loss of what could have been. I hadn't been pregnant long, but I had already come to love that little one in that ultrasound. Everyone knows what to say when you lose a parent or an uncle. But no one really knows what to say when you lose a pregnancy. You hear things like, "It's better this way" or

"Don't worry, you can have another one" or "Be thankful that you have the two you have." I'm sure all the words were meant to be soothing, but nothing really helped much. No one really has the words to express sorrow to someone who has lost what could have been.

It would hit me in waves … the sadness, I mean. I would think I was okay, but then, all of the sudden, I would become blue. I would just get sad. I couldn't really explain it. Months went by and my cousin who had been trying to have a baby finally got pregnant. When I was told the happy news, I cried. But I wasn't crying because I was so happy for her (*although I really was happy for her*), I was crying because it reminded me that my belly had never gotten big and round, and that my arms were empty. Then I would feel a weird type of guilt for not being 100 percent giddy with joy for my cousin because I felt selfish grieving for my loss. *Emotions are really confusing.*

I don't really know why these kinds of things happen. There is such mystery in loving our God. I have a huge list of questions to ask Him when I meet Him face to face. This is just another one to add to the list. However, I *do* know that in every pain we face here on earth, Jesus promises it is for our own good. I know that someday I will get to meet those little ones. I know that although they never got to run and play on this planet, they are dancing and singing with Jesus. And I'll get to see their faces and hold them on the other side. It gives me hope and anticipation. It's just one more thing to look forward to when my time comes.

~~~~

My goal is that they may be encouraged in heart and united in love, so that they may have the full riches of complete understanding, in order that they may know the mystery of God, namely, Christ.

—Colossians 2:2

Time Flies

"We're taught to expect unconditional love from our parents, but I think it is more the gift our children give us. It's they who love us helplessly, no matter what or who we are." —Kathryn Harrison, The Kiss

~~~~

TIME FLEW BY. When I was younger, older people often told me how important it was not to grow up too fast. Enjoy my youth, they said, because I would only be a child once, but an adult forever. Once my mom, with her jet-black perm, bent down to look into my eyes and tucked a strand of hair behind my ear and said, "You have so much life ahead of you." Children cannot understand the importance of those words. However, as the years past, they resonated within me.

Some seasons seemed to drag on at a snail's pace, while others seemed to be gone in the blink of an eye. When my children were younger, time seemed to stop. The days were filled with changing diapers, washing bottles, washing clothes, washing children ... and much more. Every day the hours would pass with nap times, fits, and making meals and snacks. It was my own personal "Groundhog Day." I think that's when I noticed my first gray hair! Every once and a while, someone would pat me on the hand and reassure me that this, indeed, *was* a season to enjoy because it would be over before too long. I would shake my head in appreciation of the encouragement, but roll my eyes inside because I was in the middle of a terribly emotionally draining time.

Suddenly, one day though, I found myself on the other side. I didn't even realize it had happened, but one day I woke up and we were in warp speed. With three kids, and two of whom were teenagers, they rushed in from one place and rushed out to another in a constant blur. And, I was left behind in the whirlwind's aftermath feeling my heart hurt just a bit because it was not how it used to be.

Paisley has it the worst. As the oldest, she is the first to graduate high school. I dread the springtime because I constantly see graduation commercials on TV with little girls playing in the yard one minute, and then driving off to college the next. I become a blubbering mess. It became a family joke. I hadn't always been that way. I used to be the one that didn't cry at movies very much or gush over babies. But now, I have to carry little Kleenex packets around to wipe my teary eyes. I blamed it on hormones.

I still see Paisley as the little girl with bangs that liked to play softball. How she used to stand in the doorway and gather speed to jump in the bed with us on Saturday mornings. I still feel her sweet soft cheek against my own as we hug and kiss goodnight after she told me about her day.

And, just as quickly as those days came and went, Paisley became a Godly, faithful, and beautiful young woman. She became an authentic, strong and compassionate person that I love being around. And, although I am so looking forward to what the future holds, I hope that the time we spent together when I was a young mom and she was my little girl, was all that I could've made it. I hope we had more good days than bad ones. I hope we had more laughs than we had tears. I hope she looks back with fondness. I just hope.

Now *I'm* the one saying to take it slow. *I'm* the one saying don't grow up so fast. *I'm* the older one. And, it's true. I'm learning to soak in the days like the warm sun and letting the memories imprint themselves on my soul. I am so grateful the Lord saw me fit to allow me to be a mom to these children. And, just as He was ever so capable of being with me through those slow seasons, He is with me now when I am fast-forwarding through these precious years. And, He will be there when they leave my husband and me to set out on their own adventures.

~~~~

There is a time for everything, and a season for every activity under the heavens: a time to be born and a time to die, a time to plant and a time to uproot, a time to kill and a time to heal, a time to tear down and a time to build, a time to weep and a time to laugh, a time to mourn and a time to dance, a time to scatter stones and a time to gather them, a time to embrace and a time to refrain from embracing, a time to search and a time to give up, a time to keep and a time to throw away, a time to tear and a time to mend, a time to be silent and a time to speak; a time to love and a time to hate, a time for war and a time for peace.

—*Ecclesiastes 3:1-8*

Life Lesson 8
The Power of Persistence

DON'T STOP NOW. Now, I know, it gets discouraging when we see how far we have to go. I can't count the number of times I wanted to quit. You've got challenges and roadblocks in front of you as well. The key is to keep going. Move forward, even if it is a baby step. I can tell you from personal experience that the bounce back woman never quits!

Moving On

"Rest is not idleness, and to lie sometimes on the grass under trees on a summer's day, listening to the murmur of the water, or watching the clouds float across the sky, is by no means a waste of time." —*John Lubbock,* The Use of Life

~~~~

I STARED AT a picture of my little family in its frame. We were all there: husband, wife, daughter, and son. I studied our faces, smiling and happy. Paisley with her tiny crooked teeth and Eddie with his baby baldhead look so innocent and pudgy with health. My husband and I looked full of promise. We looked like we could take on the world. True, we were young, but we had such a bright road ahead. I took a deep breath, wrapped newspaper around the picture frame, and tucked it into the moving box.

I looked around the living room and saw what seemed like hundreds of boxes stacked from floor to ceiling. I did not know how I could finish the packing. It had barely been a year since we had moved into the house. But, after all that had happened, the children and I could not stay. I couldn't afford to. *It's so unfair. It really is. What did I do to make*

*this mess? It doesn't matter, because I'm here cleaning it
up ... alone.*

It's amazing how fast circumstances can change. One day, I
thought my husband and I were just having the usual troubles, a rough spot. But, I never thought it would end in divorce. Everything went downhill at warp speed, as if a tor-
nado had struck. But it hadn't hit my house, it had hit my
heart.

I heard my children upstairs playing between the boxes
they had used to create their very own city. My heart broke
for them, too. They were too small to know the depth of the
pain, but before too long, they would know it all too well. I
wouldn't be able to hide all this forever. They thought we
were going to move in with Nini and Momo (my parents),
and that was super exciting for them. Who didn't want to
live with the most fun grandparents in the world?

Although that was years ago, I remember exactly how I
felt: like a complete failure. I had moved out of my parents'
home when I was 18 ... Miss Independent. After one terrible semester at college, I returned home to work. I got married at 19, quit work, and had two children really quickly.
And, then, at 26, I became a single mom with a high school
diploma, moving back in with her parents. *Ugh!*

I looked at the awful choices ahead of me. The choices
were labeled crappy, crappier, and crappiest. There really
wasn't an easy way out. The crappiest choice was to sell
my house and move into an apartment. I was going to have

to get a couple of horrible jobs to afford all the bills and daycare. Since I didn't have a college education, my job choices were *very* limited. The second crappy choice was to go back to school and live in family housing on campus. But that would mean moving an hour away from my support system, and my children would not only have to adjust to their dad no longer being around, but also a new community, as well as going to daycare every day. So, the least crappy choice was to sell the house and go back to school. Eventually I would get a *real* job, which could sustain us and the kids wouldn't have to go to daycare.

I am eternally grateful that my parents allowed me to move in with them. It was a major sacrifice on their part, too. They had complete freedom, empty nesters. That all changed when we moved into their home. During their nightly TV shows they heard screaming children and found cheerios in their seat cushions.

In my eyes, though, I felt like I was coming home with my tail tucked and my head bowed. I was so embarrassed that I couldn't cut it on my own. I felt like I had let my kids down. I had let *myself* down. It was the most humbling experience in my life.

However, as it turned out, the years I spent living with my parents were a special time. They were a gift to my children and me.

I didn't realize how important it would be for me to have someone to talk to that was older than five. I was able to run to the store if I needed to because other adults were home. I was able to focus on taking as many classes as I could possibly each semester (and summers, too) so I could get that degree. I couldn't have done that so easily if I hadn't had a roof over my head and my parents watching my back.

Most importantly, though, it allowed the kids and me to heal. I didn't know it at the time, but that's what I needed most. I needed to be around people who could encourage me and take some of the pressure off. The kids and I were so crushed by the divorce, and life had changed so fast; we were spinning in circles. Being with my parents allowed me to catch my breath…well, in reality, it allowed me to *start* breathing again.

I remember reading my Bible during that time, Psalms 23: "The Lord makes me lie down in green pastures." I had read that line several times in the past, but when I read it then, something struck me differently. It was the word "make." The Lord will **make** me lie down. *Have you ever tried to put an overly tired child to bed? If my kids went to bed over stimulated, they would fight it. They would kick, scream, and yell that they were NOT tired!* But I knew best. I just needed them to trust me. It was the same with the Lord. He was not gently reminding me I need to rest, He was *MAKING* me rest. And that was exactly what I needed to do … rest and focus on HIM so I could bounce back from this mess.

Sometimes our life situations are not our favorite. When we are low, we need to have faith that even though our circumstances are out of our control, our Lord knows what He is doing. He may be making you rest so you can gather strength in order to find your way. Don't fight it yelling and screaming. Lay back, breathe, and heal.

~~~~

The Lord is my shepherd, I lack nothing. He makes me lie down in green pastures, he leads me beside quiet waters, he refreshes my soul. He guides me along the right paths for his name's sake. Even though I walk through the darkest valley, I will fear no evil, for you are with me; your rod and your staff, they comfort me.

—Psalms 23 1:4

Train Ride

"The first question which the priest and the Levite asked was: "If I stop to help this man, what will happen to me?" But ... the Good Samaritan reversed the question: "If I do not stop to help this man, what will happen to him?" — Martin Luther King, Jr.

~~~~

"WHEN IS THE train going to be here?" asked Louie who anxiously watched down the tracks to get the first glimpse of it. It was his very first train ride, and it would be incredible. We were going to the top of Pikes Peak in Colorado to see one of the most majestic views our country has to offer. My whole family was excited!

While we were waiting to board the train, the children discovered food being sold nearby. I have often thought that if there is a teenage boy and food within a 50-yard radius of each other, it's over. Eddie couldn't resist the aroma of the grilled ham and cheese floating in the air, plus, he had to have a soda to wash it down. It was not lunchtime, and there was no need to buy something to eat on the train. It would probably get gooey and messy, and then our hands would be full of trash and leftovers. Plus, there was no bathroom on the train. If he downed the soda at his regular two minute pace, he would have to hold it as we snaked up the mountain. I wanted him to be focused on the views and not his full bladder.

However, because it was vacation, he won me over and I caved in against my motherly instincts. Shortly after he purchased his food, it was time to board. I cautioned him about being careful with his food and drink because the train was packed with people wanting to enjoy the view. Other tourists would not want to deal with kids and smelly food.

As soon as we found our seats, Eddie started enjoying his snack. After he opened his drink, he put in on the floor ... *with the top off!* The train started and orange soda spilled all over the floor and then slid backwards as the train ascended the mountain. *Ahhhhh! Are you kidding me?* I told him to pick up his drink and to clean up the sticky mess. He cleaned up the mess with the least absorbent napkins known to man, the kind of napkins that shouldn't even be called napkins because they just spread the mess instead of soaking it up. But that was all we had.

Afterwards, unbelievably, he placed his soda back on the floor. And ... it happened ... again. He kicked the soda with his foot, and no, the soda did not have a top on it. *How does this happen twice?* I could not wrap my brain around the fact that this was the second time he had done this.

I was beyond frustrated as I watched him looking down as the rest of his soda spilled onto the floor. We were out of napkins, and all the other passengers seated around us stared in disgust as we continued to make a complete mess. It was one of those moments, that as a parent, I wanted to drop through the floor. Since that was impossible, I asked Eddie why the cap hadn't been on the soda. He told me he didn't have enough hands to clean the mess *and* put the cap on. *Really?* It was one of those times when parenting teenagers didn't make any sense. In my most motherly way, I reminded him that when he felt as if he couldn't do it all, he should ask for help!

A little side note: At the same time this was all going on, Louie was not responding well to the altitude and decided it would be best to take off all his clothes. Perfect timing.

~~~~

Being a mom can really be a test of patience. Our children can say and do things that cause us to react in ways we never thought we would, or could, for that matter. But, watching Eddie trying to clean up his mess made me think of how the Lord sees us in all of our messes. We think we have it all together, and then BAM, a mess. He watches us fumble around, sometimes making bigger messes because we are trying to handle things on our own. We think we have it all under control. We think, *"I've got this!"* When, in reality, we couldn't be more wrong. Jesus is there with us the whole time. He is watching us use the terrible napkins. He sees that we've left the cap off. He is just waiting patiently to be asked for His wisdom and direction.

If you are in a big mess right now, whether its your own making or not, the Lord is hoping you will let Him in. He is lovingly waiting on you to call upon His name. We have the most amazing resource; all we have to do is ask.

~~~~

You may ask me for anything in my name, and I will do it.
—John 14:14

Life Lesson 9
The Power of Grace

IN ORDER TO bounce back, you've got to give yourself grace. We are not perfect, nor will we ever be. The pressure we can put on ourselves to be further along on the journey than we are can be extreme. Take time to love and accept the people we are, but at the same time, remember that we are works in progress in the Father's hands.

Liar, Liar Pants on Fire

"... what you think is right isn't the same as knowing what is right." —*E.A. Bucchianeri*, Brushstrokes of a Gadfly

~~~~~

WHEN WE ARE kids, springtime is always amazing! The school year would soon be coming to an end. The students suffered from spring fever, which even the teachers had at that time of the year. And, on top of it all, there were the yearbooks. Could it get any better?

Teachers would try to maintain control of the classes when students delivered the beautiful, shiny red books to the room. We would all turn in excitement. We had ordered them so long ago; I had nearly forgotten they were even coming. I wondered if my picture was good. I will only be in the fifth grade once. Did I have any quotes in there? Were there any snapshots that would embarrass me? This is a *forever* book. I knew I would look back on my yearbooks even when I'm old. I hope it's good! As soon as the books arrived, the room would fill with chatter. My teacher in fifth grade, Mrs. Hastings, could tell she was about to lose the attention of the class; she decided to bargain with us. If we completed our work, she would give us 30 minutes to look through the yearbooks at the end of the day. And, she would allow us to exchange books to get autographs. That was the best part.

We all settled down to live up to our part of the deal. Time seemed to crawl as we waited for the end of the day. But, sure enough, it did finally come. Our teacher called on each student one-by-one. Every time she called a name, the other students looked in awe at that lucky person. Finally my name was called. The first thing I did with it, besides write my name in the upper left hand corner, was open the book to the very middle and take a deep sniff! I have always loved the smell of a new book ... doesn't matter what kind it is. *I am not ashamed of this.*

I scrolled through the pages. I saw many friends and strangers; all looked their best for the photographer. I paged through until I found my picture. *Yeah ... it looks like what I thought it did ... darn it.* Then I looked for the club pages to try to find my picture there, too. *Are there any outtakes?*

A short time later, it was time to exchange our books I couldn't wait. I got my pen out and was ready. I knew my best friend, Meredith, and I were going to exchange first. And, I knew exactly what to write! Something so perfect that we would laugh forever. I knew she would never be able to top it! When it was time, we headed directly to one another and exchanged books with smiles plastered on our faces. The kind of smiles that communicated "You're gonna love what I've got in store for you" look. I opened her yearbook to the inside spine. I got my pen and wrote, "Thanks for letting me write in your crack." I drew a picture of a butt next to it. It looked a bit like a curly uppercase W, but I had done my best. I examined my masterpiece and laughed to myself. She loved it. We thought it was perfect ... until ...

Meredith brought her yearbook to the teacher for her autograph. I didn't even think anything of it until I saw Mrs. Hastings turn the yearbook sideways to read my inscription. *Oh no! Mrs. Hastings is reading it! She is seeing the butt I drew! No! What was I thinking? Her eyes are getting bigger and bigger. I can't look.* I looked everywhere but her direction. But, I also wanted to know what she was doing! I couldn't hold out any longer; I looked her way ... BAM! She was staring right at me. She marched right over to me and told me how disappointed she was that I would write such a thing. What a terrible choice of words. Then she said she was going to make a copy of it and send it to my parents! *NO! This is the end of me. This is it! Death by yearbook ... it's over.*

Mrs. Hastings came back with a sealed envelope, which I was to get signed by my mom and dad. That night I just couldn't do it. I thought about forging my mom's signature. *I'll just sign it and she won't have to know!* I got a pencil and did my best impression of my mom's very unique signature. I had to erase it a couple of times, but I thought I had done a good enough job.

I gave it to Mrs. Hastings the next day. I could easily tell she didn't buy the signature. *Was it because it was in pencil? Was it the eraser marks?* Who knew? At that point, I was really toast because I had a new note for my mom to sign with the old note stapled to it. Plus, Mrs. Hastings planned to call home.

All the blood rushed to my head. I got home that afternoon and put myself in my room while I awaited my doom. The sky outside had turned a lovely shade of purple and that meant she was on her way. But, as my luck would have it, my dad was in town, as well. *Yay for me (insert sarcasm).*

I heard the car pull up the driveway, and the backdoor open. I was so tense! My parents are home! They know where to look for me. I hear them coming down the hallway ... and ... there they were. Both of them ... at the same time ... terrible.

My dad told me to go pick out a switch because I was going to get a spanking. *Huh? What? Now, I have had spankings before, but with a switch? How do I even find one?* I went outside and looked and looked. It needed to be a good one, I thought. I found the most brittle, skinny branch I could find. I took it to him, and he just snapped it in half. He went out and found a real switch. A green bendy one that made that whipping noise as it sliced through the air.

We went out to the garage, and he told me to face the worktable. *Here it comes. Switch! Ouch! That really hurt!*

Switch again! The stinging of the first switch hadn't stopped, when the second was already added. Tears were flowing down my cheeks. I was so embarrassed; I was almost eleven years old and I was getting a spanking. I just wanted it to end. After a few minutes, but what felt like hours, my dad told me to relax, it's over. I loosened my grip on the side of the table. I felt the stress leave my body, and then it happened. SWITCH! What? I looked over at my dad. I felt so betrayed. How could he? And then he said one sentence:

That is what a lie feels like.

Those words still resonate within me. That is what a lie feels like ... the stinging pain of someone fooling you. The way it feels when someone you care about throws away your trust. It hurts.

That was the day I decided to stop living a life of lies. That was not the first time in my life I had lied, but I had gotten into the habit of being a *liar*.

Eventually, I understood and became so grateful that my parents loved me enough to stop me from living that way. I've made mistakes since then, but the habit was broken.

As adults, we have perfected the art of lying. We speak the most damaging words about ourselves; and the awful thing is that we start to believe it. We tell ourselves we aren't smart enough to do something, or that we aren't pretty enough compared to others. We aren't the best mom for our children, or we aren't the right wife for our husbands. We make habits of telling ourselves these lies. So sad, though: We make these lies truth when we don't recognize how they keep us down.

We are new creations in the Lord. If we have Jesus, the old *us* is gone, and the new *us* is here. When you speak lies over yourself, you are telling God He made a mistake with you. You are telling Him that His purposes cannot be fulfilled in you because you're not enough. But, that's putting your faith in YOU, not the Lord! None of us are enough, but grace covers our missing pieces, and through Jesus, we become enough to fulfill His plans for our lives. Stop allowing your words to put boundaries on what you are capable of doing. Walk in confidence in truth and grab hold of the Heavenly adventure that awaits you!

~~~~

For the Lord will be your confidence and will keep your foot from being snared.

—Proverbs 3:26

The Breakfast Casserole Mom

"Remember that the happiest people are not those getting more, but those giving more." —H. Jackson Brown, Jr.

~~~~

ONE DAY, WHEN Eddie was in middle school, he walked into the house from the bus stop and grabbed a snack. While he was preparing a glass of milk and some chips, he told me he had signed me up to make a breakfast casserole and take it to school the following week for a Christmas party. For a moment after he said it, I didn't know how to react. *What part of this child whom I have known for years thought it was okay to sign me up for a breakfast casserole?* I wasn't alone in my thought because Paisley began to laugh out loud. Eddie asked her what was so funny, and this was her exact response, "Eddie, what in the heck were you thinking? Do you even *know* mom? She's the (finger quotes inserted here) "donate paper plates, napkins or plastic cups kinda mom. She's totally NOT a breakfast casserole mom!" *Oh my gosh*! I couldn't believe my daughter said exactly what I had been thinking! However, aside from that, I didn't know how I felt about being the "paper plate mom."

In my mind, all I could think of was waking up at 5:00 in the morning, and putting together a breakfast casserole, baking it, and then whisking it off to school at 6:30 in the morning. While I was dreading this, I knew there was a momma out there that probably went to sleep in her apron, woke up with freshly applied makeup, which had miraculously appeared during the night and sang, with perfect pitch, while she made her casserole for her child's class. Then I thought of our potential situation: Eddie getting a good look at my curly, frizzy hair, wild and crazy in the morning, with my sleepy, swollen eyes, sliding around in my holey slippers, cooking his casserole in the dark because I refused to turn on the lights when it was that early. A little pinch of pain entered my heart as I thought of this. *My poor son!*

You know, there are mommas out there that truly have a gift for volunteering at their children's schools. They are the moms that help out with the PTO and always sign up to be the Room Mom in the classroom. They are always there with a smile on their faces, ready, willing and always offering assistance to both teacher and classroom. When I was a teacher, I loved this momma ... but, sadly to say, I'm NOT one. I was confessing this for the first time; this is not my gift. It stung.

However, that slight glimmer of pain passed as quickly as it came. I realized I was not the breakfast casserole mom; I had three kids in three different schools. I was doing well if they were fed and had clothes on, let alone make food for other people's kids. It's okay. There are seasons in everyone's life. At that time, my season was the "paper plate" season. But, one day, when my youngest is the only one at home, I may be the "breakfast casserole momma." While I was trying to get there, others were in that phase and could easily pick up the slack. Moms, we can't be everything to everybody, but we can show our families as much love as possible, and we don't have to do it with a breakfast casserole. We do that with our hearts.

~~~~

We have different gifts, according to the grace given to each of us. If your gift is prophesying, then prophesy in accordance with your faith; if it is serving, then serve; if it is teaching, then teach; if it is to encourage, then give encouragement; if it is giving, then give generously; if it is to lead, do it diligently; if it is to show mercy, do it cheerfully.

—Romans 12:6-8

Perfectly Imperfect

"To the people who love you, you are beautiful already. This is not because they're blind to your shortcomings but because they so clearly see your soul. Your shortcomings then dim by comparison. The people who care about you are willing to let you be imperfect and beautiful, too." — *Victoria Moran,* Lit from Within: Tending Your Soul for Lifelong Beauty

~~~~

ONE NIGHT, WHEN the kids and I drove home from dinner, we parked in the garage and walked into the dark house. "What's that noise?" Louie asked. Hummm ... what noise? The three kids and I stood looking at one another in silence trying to hear what noise he was talking about. Thud ... thud ... there it was. *Oh my gosh, what is that noise?* We followed it into the entryway and it was louder. We decided that it was coming from my bedroom, which was upstairs. We all had that terrible feeling, the feeling of dread.

I tried to convince my kids to look. *Yes, I'm that mom. I totally admit it. I'm not ashamed.* But, they weren't having it. We decided the best way to go about it was to all inspect the sound *together.* I don't know when we decided to link arms, but there we were. With our arms linked, we made our way up the stairs. We stood in the hallway and peeked into my room. It was dark; I hadn't left a light on. Paisley was at the front of our little group; we nominated her to run in and turn on the light. She made us promise that we wouldn't leave her, and we promised. She left the security of the group and bravely went into my bedroom to illuminate the situation.

Click ... the lamp was turned on. The room was quiet ... dangerously quiet. Paisley was standing by the bed, and the boys and I were squished in the doorway. We could not see anything out of place. We relaxed a little, dropping our guard. But, then I saw it. It was there on my pillow! A cardinal! A bird!

The bird and I made eye contact. It felt as if it was staring into my soul because birds and I had a past. They loved my frizzy, curly hair; it calls to them, but it also entraps them. I knew this through traumatic experience. Flashbacks of seventh grade came rushing in. Remembrances of beady black eyes and little talons suddenly filled my head.

Instantly, the cardinal flew around the room, hitting its head on the ceiling, and then flying into the window. *I wish I could say I calmly took control of the situation and made a plan to allow this caged animal to get to safety. But, no, I can't say that. Here's what I did do:*

I screamed a blood curdling, glass-breaking scream. I covered my hair with my hands, and last, but definitely the worst, I steamrolled my boys down and ran past their fallen bodies in the hallway, down the stairs, and into the kitchen to safety. *Yes, it's true. I saved myself and left the fallen behind. I'm not proud of it, but that's the story.*

Ultimately, we enabled the bird to escape the house. My children still tease me about my reaction. We all laugh about it now. They bring it up at all the best moments ... family dinners, friends' houses, meeting new people. It will live with me forever.

Life can be funny, scary, and yes, unpredictable. We put pressure on ourselves to have a perfect family, with perfect children, and perfect parents; and everyone always makes the right decisions. We hide our fears from each other. We don't let outsiders see the *real* us. And the real us is where the good stuff is. It is where the freedom lies. Plus, our children really love seeing our authentic selves. It makes them feel as if they have intimate knowledge of their parents ... like they really *know* us ... flaws and all.

The bird incident was not the only bizarre thing I've done as a parent, and, it surely won't be the last. And, although we are not perfect, we are real. And, I am truly comfortable being perfectly imperfect.

~~~~

But he said to me, "My grace is sufficient for you, for my power is made perfect in weakness." Therefore I will boast all the more gladly about my weaknesses, so that Christ's power may rest on me.

—2 Corinthians 12:9

The Bounce Back Woman's Prayer

Heavenly Father, thank you so much for the gift of my salvation. It gives me endless hope that this world is not my home, and I get to spend eternity with You.

But, sometimes, living on this planet can be really hard. I have experienced loss, shame and brokenness. During those times, You were there. You felt my despair. Help me to forgive those who have hurt me so I can move forward.

I know I'm not perfect and I've hurt others, too. Forgive me, Jesus for anything that I've done to cause pain to any-one else.

Surround me with people who love and challenge me to be-come all You have designed me to be. Help me to be avail-able to do that for others.

Thank you for loving me so much that you didn't forget about me in the valley. You never promised that it would be an easy trip, but You did promise that You would never leave me alone. And all of Your promises are true.

There are so many blessings to be had on this journey, and I don't want to waste a single day being bitter or angry. Allow me to be witness to the miracles that are around me everyday. Allow me to claim my heritage as Your daughter, and that your plans for me are amazing. Use me to encourage others and lead them to You.

Thank you for this wonderful gift of life.

Whatever I do, I want to glorify Your name. I love you.

Amen

Thank You!

To my Jesus,

thank you for loving me more than I could ever imagine. I pray this story glorifies Your name and draws people to You.

To my husband, Michael, for sharing this adventure. I couldn't have ever dreamed it would be this wonderful.

To my children, Paisley, Eddie and Louie for making life amazing in a million ways and giving me lots to write about. You all have my heart.

To my Mom and Dad, there is so much to say, it would take another book, but mostly for your unconditional love, unwavering support and belief in me ... even when I didn't believe in myself.

To my sister, Breckon, my first friend.

To Mark Gilroy, David Sams, and everyone at Keep the Faith Publishing thank you for your patience, leadership and sense of humor.

To all my girls: You know exactly who you are. I am forever blessed by each one of you and your friendship.

To my small group homies, my prayer group girls, and my gal pals on the street.

To all other family and friends who have listened, prayed, laughed, and cried throughout this journey. There is no possible way I could've done this without you.

My cup runs over.

Thank You!

About the Author

Shannon was born in Memphis, Tennessee in a family that was both musically and artistically talented. Her mother was a graphic designer and illustrator, and her father was a pioneering Christian rock musician. Since Shannon was surrounded with creativity, she tended to gravitate towards music. However, it didn't take long for her to figure out that instruments were not her thing! She played many of them, just not very well. But, she did find that she had a knack for writing songs and poetry, and was able to sharpen those skills throughout her childhood.

By 19, Shannon was working at one of the top Christian music labels, and she was writing songs for artists such as *Staci Orrico, Jaci Valesquez, Disney's Jump 5,* and more.

Shannon taught school for 8 years, and during that time was able to earn her Master's Degree in Education. She is happily married with three wonderful children.

Having gone through a traumatic first marriage, Shannon has a great passion for helping women who are hurting "bounce back" through her stories of encouragement.

Facebook: bouncebackwoman
Twitter: bouncebackwoman
Instagram: bouncebackwoman

Visit Shannon's website:
www.bouncebackwoman.com

34778714R00134

Made in the USA
Middletown, DE
04 September 2016